# THE BEST OF
# LEICESTERSHIRE

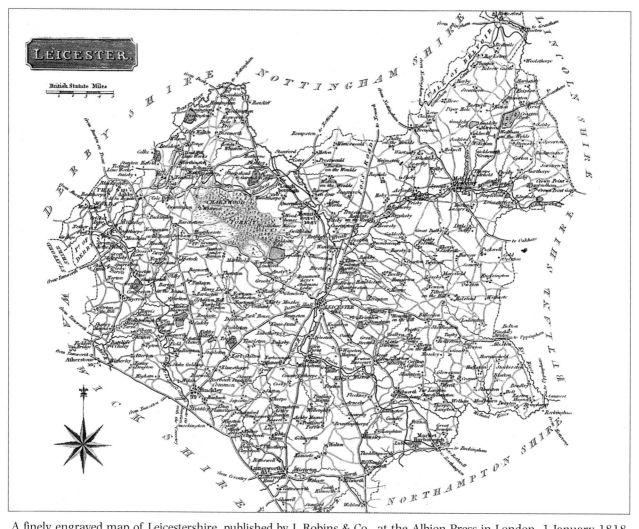

A finely engraved map of Leicestershire, published by J. Robins & Co., at the Albion Press in London, 1 January 1818. Featured on this map are major points of interest that today are of no importance. The Fosse Road enters Leicestershire at High Cross, passing Danets Hall, before running through Leicester and on to Newark. Charnwood Forest is clearly heavily wooded with Whitwick on the heathland. Coalville does not exist. Points of interest on this map in my home patch, such as Leicesterford Bridge and Crown Point, are not marked on modern Ordnance Survey maps. Leicester at that time was a small market town. According to the engraving it was little larger than Hinckley, Lutterworth, Market Harborough and Melton Mowbray.

# THE BEST OF
# LEICESTERSHIRE

### TREVOR HICKMAN

SUTTON PUBLISHING

Sutton Publishing Limited
Phoenix Mill · Thrupp · Stroud
Gloucestershire · GL5 2BU

First published 2003

*Half-title page photograph:* 'It was in the dewy valleys of the land of long ago.'
*Title page photograph*: Melton Mowbray pork pie and Stilton cheese.

**British Library Cataloguing in Publication Data**
A catalogue record for this book is available from the British Library.

ISBN 0-7509-3043-8

Typeset in 10.5/13.5 Photina.
Typesetting and origination by
Sutton Publishing Limited.
Printed and bound in England by
J.H. Haynes & Co. Ltd, Sparkford.

By the same author:

*Around Melton Mowbray in Old Photographs*
*Melton Mowbray in Old Photographs*
*East of Leicester in Old Photographs*
*The Melton Mowbray Album*
*The Vale of Belvoir in Old Photographs*
*The History of the Melton Mowbray Pork Pie*
*The History of Stilton Cheese*
*Melton Mowbray to Oakham*
*Around Rutland in Old Photographs*
*Leicestershire Memories*
*The Best of East Leicestershire and Rutland*
*The Best of Leicester*

IN GRATEFUL REMEMBRANCE OF
CHARLES BENNION
OF THURNBY IN THIS COUNTY
WHO IN THE YEAR 1928 WITH THE HELPFUL CONCURRENCE OF
THE HEIRS OF THE GREYS OF GROBY PURCHASED FROM
THEM THIS PARK OF BRADGATE AND PRESENTED IT IN TRUST
FOR THE CITY AND COUNTY OF LEICESTER THAT FOR ALL TIME
IT MIGHT BE PRESERVED IN ITS NATURAL STATE FOR THE
QUIET ENJOYMENT OF THE PEOPLE OF LEICESTERSHIRE
HIS TRUE MEMORIAL LIES AROUND

Plaque in Bradgate Park.

# CONTENTS

Introduction                                7

1.  City of Leicester                       9

2.  Hills & Forest                          15

3.  Wolds & Vale                            81

4.  Battle Plains                           109

5.  Canals & Scholars                       131

    Bibliography                            158

    Acknowledgements                        159

    Selective Index                         160

The Old Blue Boar tavern, 1838. This was the inn that Richard III slept in before the battle on Redmore Plain, 1485. Drawn by T. Flower, engraved by O. Jevitt, Leicester.

Unquestionably one of the most interesting days out in Leicestershire can be had at Conkers in the heart of the National Forest, situated on the B586 Rawdon Road, Moira, near Ashby-de-la-Zouch. On entering the reception area you meet the 'Tree of Life'. This display leads into the innovative indoor hands-on exhibition. Outside there is the assault course and adventure playpark with a miniature play area. Enjoy a short journey on the miniature railway line to the wildlife park. This park has been laid out as part of the regeneration of the area after the subsidence of underground coal faces. The park now supports shrubs and trees in an area of wetland. Sitting on the five steps on the adventure ladder are the Grechs. On the top is Simon, and descending are Amy, Sharon, Chloé and Georgina.

# INTRODUCTION

*T*he Best of Leicestershire, my third book in the series 'The Best of' by Sutton Publishing, completes the trilogy – *The Best of East Leicestershire & Rutland* was published in 2001 and *The Best of Leicester* in 2002. For three years I have endeavoured to put together a collection of photographs, drawings, engravings and paintings illustrating those places in the two counties of Leicestershire and Rutland that I consider are worth visiting. It is my selection. I have visited every place listed, with recorded history taking priority. I am not prepared to state what I consider is the most enjoyable place or town to visit. Undoubtedbly the innovative exhibitions, wildlife park and adventure playground at Conkers near Moira in the National Forest were a fine experience, especially when I had a day out at this centre with some of my grandchildren. I have always been interested in the history of the two counties, especially of the industrial revolution. To walk around Conkers, attempting to understand how this site had been developed from an extensive coal-mining area, is amazing. From pages 74 to 80 I have combined a photographic record of the past with a record of the present in the district around Moira.

Visitors need to stay in Leicestershire for a reasonable number of days or keep revisiting this splendid historic county to get a feel for the area. This book should be used as a selective itinerary. When an area of the county has been selected the visitor should contact the tourist information office. For a comprehensive selection of free leaflets and flyers contact The Tourism Section, Department of Planning and Transportation, County Hall, Glenfield, Leicester LE3 8RJ. Use this book as a general guide, with information brochures offering more specific details.

Leicestershire is a large county. For example, should any person travel from Twycross Zoo on the Warwickshire border to Belvoir Castle on the Lincolnshire border near Grantham it will take nearly two hours by car. Divide the county into four areas, similar to the chapters that I have laid out in this book. It is advisable to select particular days for your visit. Melton Mowbray has to be Tuesday – market day in one of the finest market towns in England. For industrial interest Loughborough requires at least two days, possibly three. Visit the excellent museum, and close by is the Carillon with its fine, small museums open every afternoon. The Great Central Railway requires a full day. An evening meal served in the first-class carriages is an unforgettable experience. Then there is Taylors Bell Foundry; try to join or organise a party to visit this working museum – the largest bell foundry in the world. Ashby-de-la-Zouch and Hinckley with their castles must be visited. Of course, the most important castle in Leicestershire is Belvoir Castle. Obtain a programme and enjoy a special day out there.

Leicester and every town in the county have features that are of interest, although just to drive, cycle or walk along the winding roads of Leicestershire is an experience not to be missed.

To quote G.K. Chesterton:

> Before the Roman came to Rye or out to Severn strode
> The rolling English drunkard made the rolling English road.

Then there are the canals. If time permits enjoy a trip on the Ashby Canal, taking a boat out of Sutton Cheney or Stoke Golding wharfs, along a stretch of canal that has no locks. Visit Foxton Locks on the Grand Union Canal and if possible arrange a trip from the canal basin in Market Harborough.

Park land in Leicestershire has been preserved by the county council for an increasing number of visitors. On a fresh spring day it is well worth taking the time to walk around the perimeter ramparts at Burrough-on-the-Hill, with the spread of bluebells creating a carpet of blue in the spinney along the north face of the embankment. Bradgate Park is one of the most important preserved heathlands in the country, given to the people of Leicestershire in perpetuity in 1928. Very near the park is Beacon Hill, a well preserved woodland with assorted wildlife. One of the most remarkable areas of parkland is Watermead Country Park, which was created out of disused gravel pits to the west of Thurmaston by dedicated wardens employed by the City of Leicester and Leicestershire County Council. On page 34 are four photographs of wild birds that are at home in the park, as they completely ignore their human visitors.

Good museums are always worth a visit. Some in Leicestershire are very small and are privately run by volunteers, so a small charge has to be made to maintain the exhibits. Then of course there's Snibston Discovery Park near Coalville. Any person who is interested in the history of Leicestershire must visit this museum; much more than just a museum, it is a vast educational feature on an historic coal-mining site.

All the previous books that I have compiled have been based around local history. This book is no exception. I have delved into the past, and have included many unusual historic photographs and illustrations. As I consider so much of what is in this book is *The Best of Leicestershire*, I have included many current photographs that, of course, will eventually become part of the history of this unique county.

I have enjoyed visiting every district of the county in this book. This is my personal selection based on a lifetime of interest in this area of the Midlands. I hope the reader enjoys this photographic record of a county steeped in history, and hope it will help to boost tourism in Leicestershire, so increasing the prosperity of the county.

Trevor Hickman, 2003

# 1

# *City of Leicester*

Leicester, a market town, was created a city in 1919. Essentially the City of Leicester still generates considerable interest in the Midlands for the market operating through the gateway featured above. It was designed by John Clinch and erected on 12 March 1997. In the background stands the Corn Exchange, built in 1850 by architect William Flint. The exchange was the site for buying and selling corn and of course many other commodities, not least the cheese, vegetables and fruit produced in and around farms and smallholdings in Leicestershire. Today the visitor can walk around this interesting market, viewing the variety of produce and goods that are offered for sale. A market has operated on this site for possibly over two thousand years. This short chapter only briefly features the city: for further information, read my book *The Best of Leicester*.

## ABBEY PARK

Abbey Park café with Cardinal Thomas Wolsey standing in front of the steps to the foyer. In 1530 the very ill cardinal travelled south to London on his way to meet the king. Stopping overnight at the abbey, he took to his bed, where he died on 4 November 1530.

'Give him a little earth for charity', Act iv, scene 2, line 23 from Shakespeare's *King Henry VIII*. This is possibly the site of Thomas Wolsey's grave.

The remains of Leicester Abbey in the park, where the base of the walls can be found. The abbey site was excavated in the 1920s.

CENTRE OF THE CITY

A tram passing the Clock Tower in 1905. The foundation stone for this tower was laid on 16 March 1868. John Burton and Son designed the tower. The sculptor of the four figures was Samuel Barfield. The Town Council chose Simon de Montfort, William Wigston, Sir Thomas White and Gabriel Newton to adorn this memorial.

Granby Street, 1904. This was the main route into the centre of town at the turn of the twentieth century.

## ST MARTINS SQUARE

This shopping precinct is situated close to Leicester Cathedral and the Shires shopping centre, and is bordered by Loseby Lane, Cank Street, Silver Street and St Martins Walk. This is a tasteful modern construction blending very well into the Edwardian streets encompassing this square. Interesting small shops with a fine restaurant, snack bars and tea rooms can all be found on the square, and it's all within easy walking distance of Leicester Market Place.

## CITY MUSEUMS

A view of New Walk, *c.* 1910. On the left stands New Walk Museum, which was built in 1837 as a school. It was purchased by the Corporation and converted into the town museum with support from the Literary and Philosophical Society.

Jewry Wall, 1905. Part of the Roman basilica of *c.* AD 130, this wall still stands opposite the Jewry Wall Museum which was built between 1960 and 1962 to designs by Trevor Dannatt.

## GRAND UNION CANAL

The National Space Centre dominates the skyline along the banks of the Grand Union Canal in Belgrave.

Belgrave lock on the Grand Union Canal. Visitors to Leicester should walk along the tow-path in Belgrave and enjoy the view of sites that are easily visited, such as Abbey Park, the National Space Centre and the Abbey Pumping Station.

# 2

# Hills & Forest

A lithograph drawn on stone of ruins in Bradgate Park printed for John Flower, *c.* 1820. This park is a magnet for visitors to the county. From Castle Donington in the north to Coalville in the centre of the county, there is so much that is worth seeing. The town of Ashby-de-la-Zouch has a splendid selection of small shops and its ruined castle is steeped in history. Go to Mountsorrel for the Grand Union navigation. Further along the Grand Union Canal is Watermead Country Park. In Loughborough there is the Great Central Railway and a fine museum, and the town is a centre for the casting of bells. One of the finest modern museums in the county is Snibston near Coalville, erected on the site of a disused coal mine. Nearby is Donington-le-Heath Manor House, possibly one of the oldest surviving private houses ever built in England. Any visitor to Leicestershire must visit the village of Moira where Conkers is situated in the heart of the National Forest.

## CASTLE DONINGTON

The whole area around Castle Donington is steeped in history and is a major centre for tourism, principally because of the East Midlands Airport and Donington Park. This unique three-storey tower mill, built in 1773, is seen here in the 1920s. It is controlled by a tail pole, a device that is very rare in England. It was demolished in 1940 when the site for the aerodrome was laid out. Some of the millstones were transferred to Belton water mill in 1945.

German prisoners being marched through the streets of Castle Donington in 1918 to Donington Hall, which had been converted into a prisoner of war camp. It is now the headquarters of British Midland Airways. For further reading see pages 134–8 in *Leicestershire Memories*.

Borough Street, Castle Donington, in the 1920s. Parts of this village are well worth visiting, especially the interesting antique and collectors shops.

## DONINGTON PARK

The Donington Park circuit is a splendid motor-racing track. The Spitfire memorial overlooks the start of the downhill swoop known as Craner curves, which is fast and difficult.

A view of the track going under Starkeys bridge with the 'spark plug' advertisement on the right. McLeans corner is just visible on the horizon. This magnificent race circuit for Grand Prix racing for cars and motorcycles was developed after the Second World War by Tom Wheatcroft. See page 138 in *Leicestershire Memories*.

Donington Park, 19–20 May 2001. The Vintage Sports Car Club and the Historic Grand Prix Cars Association presented 'The Return of Auto Union' at the Richard Seaman memorial trophy meeting. John Baker-Courtenay is seen here with a 1926 Sunbeam 3-litre twin-cam parked at my home on its way from North Yorkshire to attend the commemorative meeting at Donington.

A display of fine road bikes and racers; some vintage models have girder front forks.

A selection of the Vintage Sports Car Club members' cars in the Infield Park at Redgate Corner. OC 2859 is a 1933 Sunbeam 3-litre tourer. CRO 790 is a Riley 'Brooklands' style special, next to an Alvis 12/50.

An ERA R 14B with the back wheels jacked up ready to warm up the engine and transmission. These cars use a preselector gearbox and are unhappy when running in neutral; therefore it is necessary to warm up the engine in gear. Note the 'handbrake' under the near-side front wheel!

A view of the start and finish, pits and hospitality boxes. A five-lap handicap race is in progress, viewed through the safety fence behind the gravel trap at Redgate Corner.

EXHIBITION HALL

Donington Park exhibition hall. This hall is used as a venue for a variety of organisations. Any person who is interested in local history must visit The British International Collectors Fair.

IT'S A COLLECTORS DREAM
THE BRITISH INTERNATIONAL
COLLECTORS
FAIR
500 STALLS DEDICATED TO THE COLLECTOR
12th AUGUST
25th NOVEMBER
DONINGTON PARK
EXHIBITION CENTRE
CASTLE DONINGTON
(M1 J23A / 24 OR M42 / A42 J14)

Everything for the serious and amateur Collector of ~ Breweriana~Railway Relics~Guinness
Postcards~Prints~Cigarette Cards~Stamps & Coinage~Enamel Signs~Militaria~Kitchenalia
Shipping~Phonecards~Football Programmes~Bottles~Pot Lids~Early Doulton~Toys
Advertising~Badges~Ephemera~Packaging~Memorabilia from the 50s, 60s and lots more ..

FOUR IN ONE PROMOTIONS
INFORMATION: 0116 277 4396 & 0121 360 3649
em@il: fourinonepromotions@btinternet.com

A poster for the British International Collectors Fair, 2001.

Mark Bown at his postcard stall. He always has a very fine selection of postcards covering the City of Leicester and Leicestershire.

SHEPSHED

The Market Place, Shepshed, 1905, showing Henry Freeman's printers' workshop, stationers and newsagent. High in the background stands the Church of St Botolph. The vicar was the Revd William Henry Franklin Maitland.

George Gee, cyclist champion of Leicestershire, pictured with his display of trophies at the Pied Bull Hotel on Belton Street, Shepshed, 1905. The hotel landlord was William Walter Hatton.

Bull Ring, Shepshed, June 2002, formerly the Market Place. On the left is the road to Hathern via Field Street. Left of centre is Shepshed Books at 1–3 Field Street, a splendid bookshop containing a very wide selection of local history and other titles. Compare this photograph with the historic one printed at the top of page 21. There are considerable roof changes; this shop stands on the site of the double doorway to Freeman's printers.

Shepshed Market is held every Friday at Hallcroft off Field Street, with farmers' market traders. There are easy, free car parking facilities in the centre of the village.

MOUNTSORREL

Castle Hill, Mountsorrel, in an engraving published in 1757. It was the site of a Norman castle. The hill has been extensively quarried for the local granite.

Castle Hill, c. 1910. A castle was built on this hill by the Earl of Chester in about 1085. Henry II gained possession of it in 1174, and it was later held by Saer de Quincy against King John during the Barons' War of 1215. In 1217 it was held by the Earl of Pembroke against baronial mercenaries. Later the castle was besieged by Ranulf, Earl of Chester, on behalf of Henry III. In the same year, after the battle of Lincoln, the king ordered it to be destroyed.

A view of the River Soar and canal from Castle Hill overlooking the village of Mountsorrel, *c.* 1910.

Mountsorrel Granite Co. mine, 1905. Granite has been mined in this area for generations. In the 1860s the main quarry was opened and a branch railway line was laid out to convey the granite to the Midland Railway line. This mine, when at full production, employed over 700 people, working the red and grey hornblende granite to produce millstones, paving, building stone and crushed granite for road-making.

Thatched cottages on the Green, Mountsorrel, *c.* 1910. In the background stands Christ Church with its octagonal spire, erected in 1844 by Miss Brinton from local granite. The vicar was the Revd Charles Harris MA of Christ Church, Oxford.

The village market place, 1905. In the thirteenth century King Henry III granted the village permission to hold a weekly market and an annual nine-day fair starting on 10 July. This cupola was erected by Sir John Danvers Bt in about 1800.

The 'Echo Bridge' crossing the navigation, *c.* 1910. This bridge was built in 1860 to carry the mineral line conveying granite to the Midland Railway line. Before the opening of the main railway line, granite was transported in barges along canals throughout England.

The Waterside in Sileby Road, Mountsorrel, pictured here in 2001, is unquestionably a popular tourist attraction and a fine public house, originally called the Duke of York. The restaurant was converted from the stables where fresh horses waited to replace the tired horses that pulled the narrow boats on the canal.

Opening the lock gates
on the navigation on
Sileby Road,
Mountsorrel, 2001.

Chloé, Georgina,
Sharon and Amy
preparing to swing the
heavy beam on the
lock gates near the
Waterside public house,
Mountsorrel, May
2001. It is pleasant to
walk along the tow-
path by the marina and
enjoy this fine
waterway that passes
through Leicestershire.

## DISHLEY GRANGE

The medieval church of Dishley, engraved in August 1796. In this church the famous breeder of farming livestock, Robert Bakewell of Dishley Grange (1725–95), was laid to rest. Today it is a roofless ruin near a Victorian house.

Robert Bakewell was considered to be the leading breeder of livestock in the eighteenth century. He bred an improved Leicester ram and the Midland Longhorn. He made improvements in the growing and storing of arable crops. He improved the carthorse, cross-breeding it with West Friesland mares.

A Midland Longhorn, a breed originally established by Robert Bakewell. This cow is part of the Quenby Organic Longhorn herd at Quenby Hall.

## LEICESTERSHIRE COUNTY SHOW

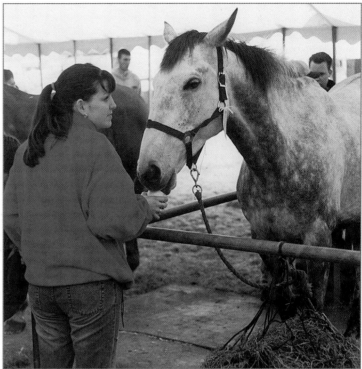

*Above:* Essentially this show revolves around agriculture, farm stock and horses, with additional entertainment and trade stands. Here one of the patient participants is having a mug of tea in the Farriers' section.

*Left:* The poster for the 161st County Show of the Leicestershire Agricultural Society. Many venues have been chosen over the past 150 years, but for the last ten years the show has been held, appropriately, at Dishley Grange.

The working hunters' ring.

The National Association of Farriers, Blacksmiths and Agricultural Engineers runs the Leicestershire Branch apprentices competition. A horseshoe is being made and fitted.

The Westerby Bassett Hounds with Master of Hounds Mrs A.E. Burton, 2002.

Taking a fence in the Hathern ring, with the funfair in the background.

Terrier racing in the main ring.

Steve Barrow, whipper-in for the Atherstone Hunt, leading the pack of hounds across the main ring.

A Bristol 25 caterpillar tractor in the Kegworth Vintage Ploughing Club parade in the main ring.

The Royal Marines Commando Display Team preparing to demonstrate their skills in the main ring.

## WATERMEAD COUNTRY PARK

For over one hundred years, certainly from the turn of the twentieth century, this valley of the River Soar, some 2 miles long, was the site of extensive gravel extraction which resulted in the formation of many flooded areas. It is now Watermead Country Park, stretching from Red Hill at Birstall through to Wanlip. In many of the excavated gravel pits the remains of long-dead mammoths were uncovered. This statue was erected in memory of the previous occupiers of this valley. Constructed in concrete by the artist Dan Jones, it was unveiled on 29 March 2001.

A visitor from North America is the Canada goose, now at home in all the ponds in the park. Here a pair are caring for their goslings.

Swans, geese, mallards and Canada geese waiting to be fed in the car park area off the A607 at the Rushey Mead/ Thurmaston site.

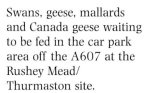

Thurmaston Lock on the Grand Union
Canal in Watermead Country Park.

The basin and boatyard off the
Grand Union Canal at Thurmaston.

A speed-boat on the watersports lake near Wanlip.

King Lear's Lake. According to local legends Lear was a
king in the eighth century BC and is buried in the Soar
Valley downstream from the city of Leicester. Shakespeare's
tragedy *King Lear* is based on this myth. In this sculpture
King Lear mourns his daughter Cordelia who was hanged
by an officer of Edmund. The Earl of Kent and the Duke of
Albany look on.

Mallards dipping.

'Harry Heron.' A grey heron has eaten a large lunch of newts and is walking home to rest!

A female mute swan on her nest.

A great crested grebe on her nest.

## BRADGATE PARK

An engraving of Bradgate
House by J.P. Malcolm,
published in 1794. The house
was built from brick between
1490 and 1505 by Thomas
Grey, Marquess of Dorset. Lady
Jane Grey was born in this
house in October 1537. The
nine-day 'queen', she was
executed in 1554 at the age of
sixteen. The Grey family
abandoned the house in the
1730s. Neglected, it became a
ruin.

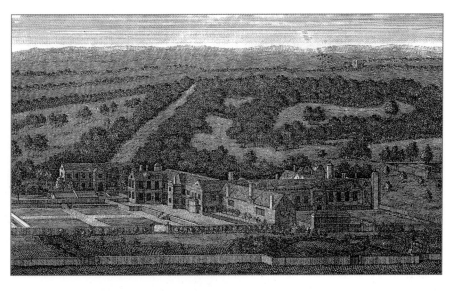

The stone bridge across the River Lin
with the ruins of Bradgate House in
the background, *c.* 1910.

Along the banks of the River Lin.
This park was given by Charles
Bannion in 1928 in Trust for the
City and County of Leicestershire,
for quiet enjoyment for the people
of Leicestershire in perpetuity.

Bradgate Park
with the ruins,
an engraving by
R. Throsby,
1796.

Bradgate House ruins with part of the
house still occupied, 1791.

The River Lin, *c.* 1910. In 1554, when
Lady Jane Grey lost her head, the foresters
employed on the estate topped all the oak
trees in the park. Some of these pollarded
oaks survived for centuries. This is a dying
oak more than 350 years after the event.

This is an interesting engraving by J.P. Malcolm, published in 1792, six years after 'Old John' was built as an eye-catcher in 1786 by the Earl of Stamford in memory of his retainer John. John liked his ale, so it was built to resemble a beer mug, on the site of a former windmill. It may have used the tower of the original windmill.

I am standing in front of 'Old John', 2002. Battlements had obviously been added. The Earl of Stamford's retainer was killed at a bonfire celebrating the coming of age of the earl's grandson.

Red deer grazing in the bracken. The park retains well over three hundred deer; during the winter months the keepers supply the herds with hay.

Fallow deer grazing in the damp area of grassland near the ruins of the hall.

Cropston reservoir viewed from Bradgate Park, *c.* 1920. This reservoir, completed in 1870, was built to provide water for Leicester. The flooded valley covered twelve farms and the head gamekeeper's house in Bradgate Park. Today it is a marvellous site to view wild birds on the reservoir from selected positions on the walls built in the park.

A waterfall, known as Little Matlock, on the River Lin in Bradgate Park, *c.* 1930.

To the Glory of God and in memory of those gallant Leicestershire Yeomanry who fell in the First World War. A further plaque was added in memory of all officers, warrant officers and men of 153 and 154 (Leicestershire Yeomanry) Field Regiments RA who fell in the Second World War. This monument was unveiled on 19 July 1927 by Lieutenant General Sir Charles Kavanagh KCB in memory of the Leicestershire (Prince Albert's Own) Yeomanry.

Having walked through Bradgate to enjoy a splendid lunch at the Grey Lady, just out of the park where the memorial to the Leicestershire Yeomanry stands high on the hill, Don and I enjoy a well-earned rest after walking across the park from Newton Linford on a very blustery spring day in 2002.

## ASHBY-DE-LA-ZOUCH

An engraving of the Market Place, 1827. On the left is the Bulls Head Inn. In the centre background stands the market cross, consisting of eight columns with an octagonal roof. During the night of 21 December 1822 Mr Mammatt, steward to the lord of the manor, encircled the columns with chains and with a team of shire horses demolished this historic structure.

Market Street, c. 1920. On the left is Holdram's ironmonger's and Charles Leonard Wykes' haberdasher's. Centre left in the background is The Star Tea Co. Ltd, importers and provision merchants. The vehicle in the centre of the street is attracting considerable interest.

The Ashby, Leicester & Burton station on the Midland Railway, *c.* 1895. It was opened on 1 March 1849 as Ashby station. The stationmaster was Alfred Everett. Here, a pair of Midland 2–4–0s are entering the station and passengers are waiting to board the train. This station was renamed as Ashby-de-la-Zouch by the Midland Railway Co. in 1923. It closed as a station on 7 September 1964.

The very first Burton and Ashby tram, car number 13, outside the Royal Hotel, 1906.

The parish church of St Helen's, 1910. The vicar was the Revd Herbert Edward Sawyer.

The chancel of St Helen's, *c.* 1910.

A drawing and photograph of the finger pillory, taken before the First World War. A form of punishment, it has thirteen grooves to take fingers of various sizes. One finger from each hand would have been inserted in a bent position, then the hands secured in place by a hinged beam. Exhibited in the parish church, it was used instead of the stocks to punish disorderly church goers.

The Royal Hotel, *c.* 1910. Built between 1826 and 1827 by Robert Chaplin, until the late 1830s it was known as the Hastings Hotel. It was erected to support the famous spa when the Ivanhoe baths were a feature of the bathing rooms in this hotel, also designed by Robert Chaplin and opened in 1822, in the first phase of this development.

The interior of the Royal Hotel, *c.* 1904. Ashby-de-la-Zouch was a major tourist attraction in the Victorian period when the nobility visited to 'take the waters'.

Ashby-de-la-Zouch Baptist Sunday School's float commencing the parade through the town from the railway station yard, 22 June 1911. The float depicts Britannia.

The Bull's Head Inn in Market Street, 1904. The landlord was Edmund Burdett. This historic building still stands in the town, though it has been subjected to a careful modernisation programme.

The Bulls Head, June 2002. Unquestionably the interior of this ancient pub has retained much of its medieval character and is well worth visiting for a midday meal. I am standing with Jo Humberston on the steps to the bar entrance of this fine old public house.

## ASHBY-DE-LA-ZOUCH CASTLE

This colour-wash was published in 1915 by Charles Ashdown, detailing his interpretation of Lord Hastings Tower, 1476; the kitchen, *c.* 1350; the pantries and buttery; the great hall, twelfth century; the chapel, fourteenth century; and other features such as St Helen's Church within the moat and the entrance to the keep.

John Flower, the Leicester artist and local historian, visited the ruins of this castle in the 1820s.

The castle's chapel in the 1790s.

The tower of St Helen's, 2002.

John Flower produced this view of the castle in the 1820s, with the parish church of St Helen's in the background.

Ashby-de-la-
Zouch Castle in
a view by John
Burton & Sons,
1890s.

An
advertisement
for John
Burton & Sons.

An aerial view of
the chapel from
the top of the
Hastings Tower,
2002.

The elaborate chimney piece in the ruined Queen Mary's room in Ashby-de-la-Zouch castle, *c.* 1910.

*Left:* Doorway and entrance to the banqueting hall in the castle, *c.* 1910.

*Right:* Inscriptions on the stone walls near the top of the Hastings Tower, 2002.

## MARKET & MUSEUM

Ashby-de-la-Zouch market, built in 1856.

The market in 2002, containing a variety of stalls. Wander in and out of the stalls and have a cup of tea in the delightful market café.

Ashby-de-la-Zouch museum. This small museum situated on North Street is open during the spring and summer months.

## COALVILLE

A small section of the map drawn and published by John Prior, master of Ashby-de-la-Zouch Grammar School, in 1777. Clearly indicated is the junction where the road from Whitwick to Hugglecote crosses. This is Long Lane where Coalville was built. Nearby is the village of Snibston, which is worth visiting to view the chapel of St Mary.

London Road, Coalville, 1903. Christ Church was built between 1836 and 1838 by H.I. Stevens of Derby. The vicar was the Revd Frederick George Copeland.

Belvoir Road, 1904. Lloyds Bank is on the corner, manager Walter Cecil Tomlinson, and the Theatre Royal, managed by Sydney Vereker, can also be seen.

Aerial view of Coalville in the late 1920s. When this photograph was taken the town had existed for about one hundred years. Coalville House was built on Long Lane in anticipation of the opening of Whitwick Colliery in 1822. The town square with the splendid Clock Tower, designed by Henry Collings and unveiled in 1925 in memory of those killed in the First World War, can be seen here.

John Goulson Watch-maker of 42 Belvoir Road photographed this parade in 1916 which was held in aid of a proposed Coalville hospital.

The Market Place and the Old Red House Inn, 1904. The landlord was Arthur William Tyler.

The centre of Coalville is marked by this splendid war memorial. It was unveiled on Saturday 31 October 1925 at 2.30 p.m. by Mrs Charles Booth from Gracedieu Manor, in the presence of ten thousand people. The 68ft-high brick tower was originally erected to the memory of the men from the Coalville area killed in the First World War. Their names were recorded in lead letters on polished Cornish granite. Subsequently in 1946 the names of those killed during the Second World War were added to the memorial.

Coalville is a modern town: it did not exist during the first part of the nineteenth century. As the years passed, so the town grew. In the twenty-first century the modernisation continues. Today it is a small but progressive, industrial town with local market interest. This is the Belvoir shopping centre, a twentieth-century retail complex in an interesting town.

A traditional miners' public house, 2002, situated in the centre of Coalville. It was built in 1836 by Thomas Coldwell.

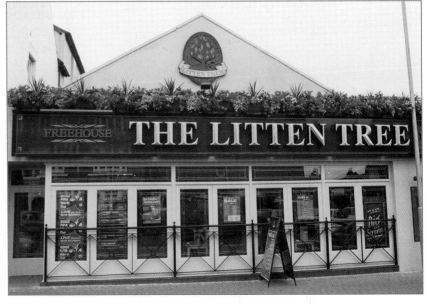

All smart, small towns have modern restaurant facilities. The Litten Tree on Marlborough Square near the modern shopping complex, shown here in June 2002, has a good restaurant serving fine food.

## SNIBSTON

The chapel of St Mary, drawn by J. Pridden and engraved by F. Cary, published on 23 May 1795. This is a fascinating small church that was considerably altered in 1847 when narrow lancet windows were built into the medieval walls. There is evidence, uncovered in 1930, that the original church, possibly built in the twelfth century, supported a tower.

Snibston No. 2 Colliery, sunk in 1833 by George Stephenson, was closed in 1983. On this site off Long Lane Snibston Discovery Park was developed.

Part of the remains of Robert Stephenson's railway, which was laid out in 1833 to take coal to Leicester from the Coalville area. This view is looking from Jackson Street towards the pit head at Snibston No. 2.

## SNIBSTON DISCOVERY PARK

The skyline in the car park at Snibston Discovery Park. This is a splendid museum and considerable time is needed, especially with children and teenagers, to take in all the exhibits and hands-on features. These two pages show only a very small selection of all that is on display in the museum.

*Left:* A working skeleton on a bike that cycles in unison with the 'living cyclist'!

*Right:* The rear of a carrier's cart. Such vehicles operated out of most villages in Leicestershire from the seventeenth century to the early part of the twentieth.

*Below:* No. 2 engine from Ellis & Everard's Markfield and Bardon Hill granite quarries.

Left: Pack horses, such as the one in this fine display, would probably have been used to convey produce and materials around what is now Leicestershire, for perhaps two thousand years or more.

Right: The manufacture of 'granite setts'. For well over two hundred years small blocks of granite from Leicestershire were used for pavement surfaces. Mountsorrel granite is now used as crushed stone in tarmac.

Above: If possible, join one of the conducted tours of Snibston No. 2 pit head, such as this one in June 2002. Brian Hinsley is describing in graphic detail how this coal mine was worked, until it closed in 1983. Brian worked at the pit head from the age of fifteen, and his talk and tour is one of the finest one-hour discussions I have heard in any museum I have ever visited.

Right: Snibston No. 2 pit head, with the discovery park water features, on a warm sunny day.

## DONINGTON-LE-HEATH

The farmhouse at Donington-le-Heath, seen here in a drawing by J. Pridden, dated 23 May 1795, and engraved by F. Cary, is one of the oldest houses in England. Built in about 1290 as a manor house, it was later let to various tenant farmers. Unfortunately by the 1950s it had become derelict and was used as a pigsty. In 1966 the restoration of the house commenced when Leicestershire County Council purchased the building. Some of the timbers used in 1290 are still incorporated in the building today.

Simon Grech with his mother Carmelina in the herb garden laid out at the manor house. Carmelina, a Maltese historian, visited the historic structure in April 2002. She is also the author of *Old Photographs of Malta*, Sutton, 1999.

The sixteenth-century kitchen of the farmhouse at Donington-le-Heath with its large fireplace, April 2002. A selection of items used in this type of kitchen are on display. Georgina is standing inside the archway.

This bed has been considerably altered since August 1485 when King Richard III slept in it in Leicester. In 1580 the original bed collapsed and in a drawer under the bed coins to the value of £300 were found. The bed was rebuilt in the Elizabethan style, but how much of the original timber was reused is unknown. See page 151 of *Leicestershire Memories*.

A display featuring the lady of the house with a spinning wheel, with Georgina looking on. The staff of Donington-le-Heath museum put on many educational exhibitions and weekend displays, and arrange visits for schoolchildren and students to extend their knowledge of local history.

## LOUGHBOROUGH

A 1930s photograph of the Town Hall and Market Place. The licence to hold a market in the town was granted in 1221. Traditionally market days are Thursdays and Saturdays. The Borough of Charnwood has backed a campaign to attract tourists to the town with considerable finance obtained from numerous sources. Spend some time in this historic town. I would estimate that you need at least three days, as a visitor, to take in all that is available during the summer months.

The Great Central Hotel, c. 1910. It is situated near the Great Central Railway station and only a short distance from Taylors Bell Foundry. Book a visit to the Bell Foundry and then take a trip on the steam line of the Great Central Railway.

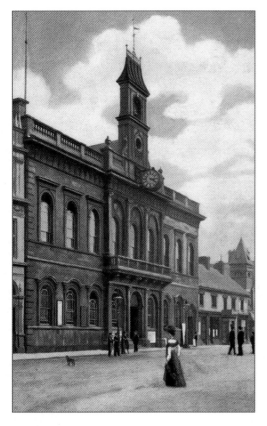

*Left:* The Town Hall in an oil painting of 1905, printed and marketed for the tourist trade.

*Right:* The Bull's Head Hotel sign displayed across High Street in 1904. The landlord was Edwin Lewis Meadows. Signs such as this have their origins in gibbets erected across the road. Highway robbers, especially those who had stolen the king's post, were hung up on display as a deterrent to others.

The Market Place, 1905. On the left is W. Armstrong & Son's furnishing warehouse. In the background is the Lord Nelson public house at 35 Market Place. The landlord was J. Gutteridge.

## ALL SAINTS' CHURCH

All Saints' Church in an oil painting printed and marketed in 1905. A thirteenth-century building, it has been considerably altered over many centuries. All Saints' is constructed in the Decorated and Perpendicular styles. Visit this historic church and spend some time examining the record of the past that is on display in this splendid building.

The nave looking towards the chancel in All Saints' Church, 1920s. Considerable changes took place in this area of the church in the 1960s.

All Saints' Church viewed from the top of the Carillon in the summer of 2002.

## THE MARKET

The Market Place with the Town Hall in the background, *c.* 1910.

Michael Walker selling his famous Stilton cheese at the Farmers' Market in 2002. The market is held in Devonshire Square near the Town Hall on the second Wednesday of every month.

## CHARNWOOD MUSEUM

Charnwood Museum in Queens Park on Granby Street is one of the best small museums in Leicestershire. It is a very fine educational facility with many good exhibits. Opened as a museum on 10 August 1998, it was originally built as the town's baths in 1897. Three very different displays are shown on these two pages. During the summer months you can enjoy a cup of tea on the museum terrace.

A Bronze Age burial. This is a reconstruction of a grave found near Cossington on an archaeological dig. It shows the remains of an eight-year-old boy who died nearly 4,000 years ago. It is presumed this is how he was clothed when his body was buried. Pottery vessels and implements were placed with the body, as they were considered essential in the afterlife.

Dig for Victory! Land Army girls worked on the land during the Second World War.

An Auster aeroplane suspended from the ceiling in the museum. This plane was made by Auster Aircraft Ltd at the village of Rearsby in 1947. It was one of 3,800 such planes that were built during the years 1939 to 1968 principally for the army. This plane is G-AJRH, winner of the 1956 King's Cup air race. See page 49 in part one of *The Melton Mowbray Album*, Sutton, 2001.

## TAYLOR'S BELL FOUNDRY

*Left:* Taylor's Bell Foundry in Freehold Street, Loughborough, is the largest bell foundry in the world.

*Right:* The Bell Foundry Museum is well worth visiting to learn about the history of bell manufacture. A tour of the works is a unique experience, but this must be pre-arranged with the curator.

Inside the Bell Foundry. For over 200 years bells have been cast in Taylor's Foundry, including Great Paul that hangs in St Paul's Cathedral; at over 16 tonnes, it is the largest bell in Great Britain. On the right is the outer mould used for casting Great Paul.

*Left:* A selection of bells with new castings and very old bells that have been retuned. The Taylor family had already started a bell foundry in St Neots, Huntingdonshire, by 1786. The family moved to Loughborough in 1838.

*Right:* Casting bell crowns in the foundry, June 2002.

Bells being tuned by hand and also on a vertical bore, left. Bells produce more than one note when struck, but the overall sound should harmonise.

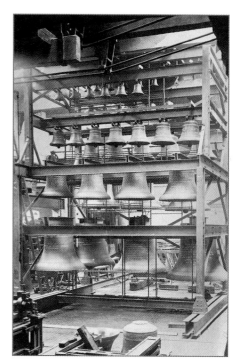

Loughborough war memorial, Carillon and museum in Queens Park, *c.* 1925. The Carillon was built through local subscriptions, and the foundation stone was laid by General Lord Horne on 22 January 1922. The first recitals were delivered on 22 July 1923 by a *carilloneur* from Belgium. The tower is 15ft high and there are 47 bells with a total of 138 steps. Three floors are laid out as a small museum, started by volunteers in 1981.

The Carillon bells being built by Taylor's Bell Foundry in 1922.

The 47 bells were dedicated by numerous people and organisations. This bell records Peter Sellars of the 6th Leicestershire Regiment.

Turret, roof and balcony were built from oak encased in copper. During the season it is open from 1 p.m. each day and is manned by volunteers.

The dedication on the tower, which was built in memory of the 480 Loughborough men killed in the First World War, now also commemorates those killed in the Second World War.

## GREAT CENTRAL RAILWAY

Entrance and ticket room. Enjoy a day out on Britain's only main line steam railway. It is a living museum, an ongoing record of the past. Visit the sheds and view the fantastic trains being rebuilt.

British Rail no. 90775 in steam about to leave for Rothley, Quorn and Leicester North station, off Red Hill Way.

Dining in style is to be recommended! Take a step back in time and enjoy a four-course meal while travelling by steam train. Lorna Maybery is enjoying her starter in the first-class dining car during a Saturday summer's evening excursion. To book a table contact Loughborough (01509) 230726.

## BEACON HILL

*Left:* The beacon on Beacon Hill. This hill is of archaeological importance and archaeological surveys are always being done. The country park comprises approximately 335 acres and at its highest point it is 802ft above sea level. Visitors can walk through the park's well-maintained woodland and view assorted wildlife.

*Above:* The Old Man of Beacon Hill. As far back as 700 million years ago this hill was formed when volcanic eruptions deposited a layer of ash at the bottom of an ancient sea. About 600 million years ago intense geological activity caused the strata to buckle, resulting in the present characteristic landscape around Charnwood Forest.

Park rangers maintain the heathland and spinneys. During the summer months they encourage rare breeds of sheep, such as these Ronaldsay sheep, to graze the bracken, so as to encourage certain other plants that grow on the heath to develop.

## STAUNTON HAROLD

Staunton Harold Hall and church, *c.* 1790. In 1760 this hall became famous for the murder of John Johnson, steward to Earl Ferrers, who was shot dead by his employer in a fit of rage. The earl was later executed at Tyburn.

The hall and church from the lake, 1904.

A contemporary wood engraving, published in April 1760, showing Earl Ferrers being executed at Tyburn (now the site of Marble Arch). At his trial in the House of Lords, he was quickly found guilty. He was sentenced to be hanged and disembowelled at Tyburn, and his remains were to be left on display for five days.

*Left:* The Right Hon. Earl Ferrers MA, JP, DL, 1895. He was a direct descendant of Earl Ferrers of Staunton Harold who was hanged at Tyburn.

*Right:* The picturesque garden entrance to Staunton Harold Hall, June 2002.

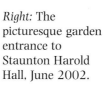

FERRERS CENTRE

Ferrers' heraldic animals at the entrance to the Centre near the church and the hall on the drive down past the lake.

The main entrance to the Ferrers Centre. Off the courtyard are sixteen workshops which feature a variety of crafts such as stone carving, ceramics, textiles, sign writing, jewellery, restoration of porcelain and blacksmithing.

The Georgian courtyard at the Ferrers Centre with the tea and luncheon rooms.

CONKERS AT MOIRA

The Marquis Pit, the colliery near Moira station, part of Moira Colliery Co. Ltd, 1910.

A Moira coal wagon on track at Moira Colliery Co. Ltd, Ashby-de-la-Zouch, 1918.

Rawden colliery near Moira station, 1918.

The coal mines have all gone now. Part of the National Forest has replaced the 17 square miles of coalfields. Now we have Conkers in the heart of the National Forest, opened in 2001.

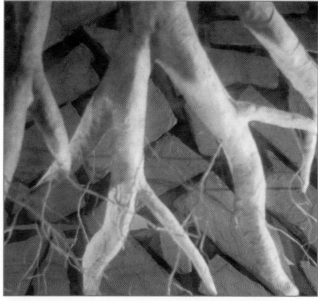

The roots of the 'living tree' in the foyer at Conkers. This tree is symbolic of all that the National Forest stands for.

Conkers Discovery Centre in front of the
maintained lake, spring 2002.

The famous Round House at Moira Bath
colliery, 1918.

Moira Bath colliery with the saw mill and wood yard, 1918.

The collieries have gone, to be
replaced with an activity trail,
possibly where the coal headings
used to be situated.

An overhead activity, spring
2002.

The adventure playground for
young children near the lakeside
restaurant, 2002.

Moira wagons at the Rawdon colliery sidings, 1918.

The Conkers train link arriving at the waterside from the discovery centre, 2002.

*Marquis* on track at Rawdon in 1918.

Ashby Canal basin near the
lakeside restaurant at Conkers,
2002.

The Ashby Canal at the Moira Bath colliery,
1918.

During the reopening of the length of the
Ashby Canal that runs through Moira, a
road bridge was built with a set of locks
because of subsidence through mining.
The Ashby Canal was completed in 1804.
It ran from the north of Moira to the
Coventry Canal, 30 miles away, without
encountering any locks. The top 8 miles
were closed in 1966 because of subsidence.
A scheme is in progress to open up the
canal from Conkers in the heart of the
National Forest, through to the Coventry
Canal at Marston, so allowing tourist boats
to be moored in the basin at Conkers.

## MOIRA FURNACE

The magnificent locks at Moira, 2002. They were built on the canal leading from Moira furnace to the Conkers basin.

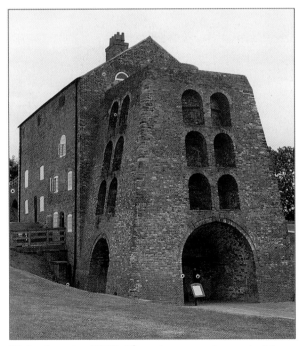

Moira furnace, 2002. There is an ongoing project to open up the whole length of the Ashby Canal for tourism, part of a wider plan for economic and environmental improvement of the surrounding area.

The Ashby Canal connects the Moira furnace to the basin at Conkers via the locks shown above.

# 3
# Wolds & Vale

Unquestionably the finest stately home open to the public in Leicestershire is Belvoir Castle. Standing on the escarpment, it dominates the Vale of Belvoir and the Leicestershire to Lincolnshire Wolds. Restoration of the house, which was partially destroyed by fire in 1816, resulted in this 'fairytale castle'. John Flower, the Leicester-based artist and local historian, produced this drawing in the 1820s, during the restoration. Under the direction of the Revd Sir John Thoroton, the exterior was finally completed in 1830. I feature four sites in this chapter, complementing the selection published in some of my previous Sutton books. The first part concentrates on the area in and around Belvoir Castle, to be followed by the town of Melton Mowbray. Burrough-on-the-Hill is included once more. This selection does not cover every interesting place that is worth visiting in this area. The reader must read my books *The Best of East Leicestershire & Rutland* and *The Best of Leicester*.

BELVOIR CASTLE

The 'Castle on the Hill' viewed from the Vale. See pages 39–45 in *The Best of East Leicestershire & Rutland.*

Her Grace the Duchess of Rutland and Peter de Saumarez sitting in the historic gardens, May 2001. In the gardens outside the west wall of the castle is a fine display of sculptures in the restored Rose and Statue Gardens.

The Rose and
Statue Gardens,
with the castle in
the background.
For further
reading see pages
2–32 in *The Vale
of Belvoir in Old
Photographs*.

A peacock on
display is the
emblem on the coat
of arms of the
Dukes of Rutland.

## SPRING GARDENS

The Summer House in the Spring Gardens on the Duke's Walk, *c.* 1910. This woodland garden was started in 1800 by the 5th Duchess of Rutland. She dispatched her agents around the world to purchase rare and unusual trees, shrubs and plants that could survive in this woodland in north Leicestershire.

The restored Summer House, June 2001. Many of the shrubs and trees planted by the 5th Duchess have survived and matured. In June 1970 the Duchess of Rutland began restoring the existing garden. It took her twenty-five years to select and plant new trees, shrubs and plants.

The restored arch above
the Summer House,
2001.

Visitors listening to a talk
being delivered by the head
gardener, June 2001.

Spring Gardens, June 2001.
The woodland garden lies in
a natural amphitheatre, fed
from a freshwater spring –
hence the name. Water rises
from a fissure in the rocks
that make the escarpment on
which stands the castle.

## SIEGE OF BELVOIR CASTLE

The castle at peace,
27 May 2001.

'The Siege Group' in
camp near the castle,
2001.

'The Siege Group' attacking Belvoir Castle, 27 May 2001. During the English Civil War the castle was under siege, but it was never taken by storm. The Earls of Rutland were Parliamentarians. However, during the 8th Earl's absence the castle was occupied by Royalist forces from Lincolnshire, who held out against the attacking Parliamentarians for four years.

Royalists defending the castle.

Parliamentarians attacking the castle.

Royalists suffering under the attack.

Parliamentarians storming the ramparts.

The Royalists' surrender in 2001 – an event that
never happened during the English Civil War.

## THE QUEENS ROYAL LANCERS

In the castle is a splendid regimental museum. The Queens Royal Lancers Regiment was formed in 1993 as an amalgamation of several historic units, including 16th/5th The Queens Royal Lancers, 21st Lancers, and the 17th/21st. Undoubtedly the most famous regiment is the 17th Lancers, the 'Death or Glory Boys'. As part of the Light Brigade they charged at Balaklava in the Crimean War in 1854.

This is Bill Brittain's bugle that sounded the famous charge.

### 'THE CHARGE OF THE LIGHT BRIGADE'

I    Half a league, half a league,
Half a league onward,
All in the valley of Death
Rode the six hundred.
'Forward, the Light Brigade!
Charge for the guns!' he said;
Into the valley of Death
Rode the six hundred.

II    'Forward, the Light Brigade!'
Was there a man dismay'd?
Not tho' the soldier knew
Some one had blunder'd:
Their's not to make reply,
Their's not to reason why,
Their's but to do and die:
Into the valley of Death
Rode the six hundred.

III    Cannon to right of them,
Cannon to left of them,
Cannon in front of them
Volley'd and thunder'd;
Storm'd at with shot and shell,
Boldly they rode and well,
Into the jaws of Death,
Into the mouth of Hell
Rode the six hundred.

IV    Flash'd all their sabres bare,
Flash'd as they turn'd in air,
Sabring the gunners there,
Charging an army, while
All the world wonder'd:
Plunged in the battery-smoke
Right thro' the line they broke;
Cossack and Russian
Reel'd from the sabre-stroke
Shatter'd and sunder'd.
Then they rode back, but not,
Not the six hundred.

V    Cannon to right of them,
Cannon to left of them,
Cannon behind them
Volley'd and thunder'd;
Storm'd at with shot and shell,
While horse and hero fell,
They that had fought so well
Came thro' the jaws of Death
Back from the mouth of Hell,
All that was left of them,
Left of six hundred.

VI    When can their glory fade?
O the wild charge they made!
All the world wonder'd.
Honour the charge they made!
Honour the Light Brigade,
Noble six hundred!

Alfred, Lord Tennyson

War proves very little, and great sacrifices are made by very brave men. One of the bravest was the 7th Earl of Cardigan. He led the charge from the front: 673 mounted men charged and over-ran the Russian guns. In the attack 247 Lancers were killed and 500 horses were slain. Cardigan survived and came back to Leicestershire to live on into retirement at Brooksby Hall near Melton Mowbray.

PICNIC CONCERTS

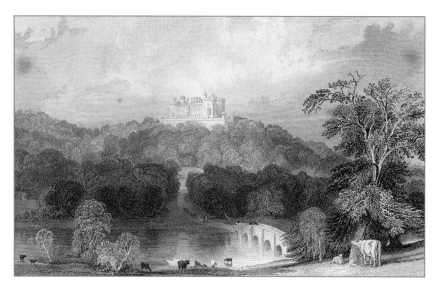

The lake, bridge and Belvoir Castle, now the site of many open-air concerts, in a drawing by T. Allan, published in 1836.

The lake, dairy and Belvoir Castle at the start of one of the picnic concerts in the grounds of Belvoir Castle, 21 July 2001.

'The Great Master of the Clarinet' Acker Bilk on the open-air stage at the picnic concert.

Mary and Pam reading their programmes at the picnic concert.

'The Welsh Diva' Shirley Bassey on stage at the picnic concert which was attended by ten thousand people.

The closing display of fireworks at the end of the open-air concert.

## BELVOIR CASTLE RAILWAY

William Jessop, the canal engineer, in consultation with the 5th Duke of Rutland, designed and constructed an edge railway with flanged wheels. The 4ft 7½in-gauge track was set and spiked down on stone blocks. The rail was fitted as a double track and the line was opened in 1793 to convey coal in horse-drawn wagons to the castle from the Grantham Canal.

Belvoir Castle edge railway, 1901. This railway ran from Muston Gorse to the castle and much of the track was uphill. A reversing brake is clearly visible on this wagon. This prevented weary horses being dragged backwards, when they rested on the way up the hill.

Alan Salt, promotions historian, examining remains of the edge railway that still crosses the road near the castle, July 2002.

A surviving wagon on the edge railway in the tunnel that was built under and into the castle in 1815. The railway was 3 miles long and was worked for 107 years from 1793 to 1901.

## MELTON COUNTRY PARK

A view of the low valley leading to Scalford from Melton Mowbray, April 1971. Melton Country Park was laid out in these fields.

A similar view of the same area, 2002.

Melton Country Park visitor centre off Wymondham Way, 2002. For information on the Country Park visit this centre, where there are brochures and flyers and a good display of photographs.

## MELTON MOWBRAY

The Church of St Mary's, 1905. It is undoubtedly the finest church in Leicestershire.

Craven Lodge was built in 1827 by Dr Keal. It was purchased by the Hon. W.G. Craven in 1856 who extended the building. In 1922 it was purchased by Capt Michael Wardell who divided the house into several fine apartments to be let to the fox-hunting fraternity. In 1923 the Prince of Wales took one of the apartments.

Fox hunting was big business in the nineteenth century and into the first half of the twentieth century, up until the outbreak of the Second World War. The Prince of Wales, later King Edward VIII, had Craven Lodge as his autumn and spring residence for sixteen years, and entertained his mistresses there. The eight stables are situated at the rear of the residence.

## MELTON STREET MARKET

The street market on Nottingham Street, 1905. On the right stands the Half Moon public house. The landlord was George Stephens. Today this is still an excellent public house, especially busy on market day.

The George Hotel, High Street, 1905. The landlord was Henry William Sampey. Today the street market is held in front of this hotel. The carriage entrance to the rear of the hotel no longer exists. This is probably a posed photograph; the carriages at the front of the hotel could have come from the stables at the rear of the premises.

Melton Mowbray Market Place with the Tuesday market in full swing, 1904. On the left are the premises of Frederick Warner, manufacturer of the famous Melton Mowbray pork pie. Centre background is the shop of Arthur Eagers, boot maker to the hunting fraternity. Miss Emma Goddard, draper, had her main shop at 13 Burton Street.

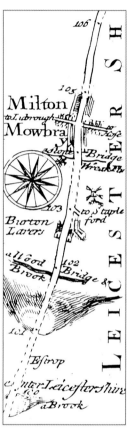

An extract from the first road atlas by Emmanuel Bowen, 1720. The Leeds to London route was used by the stage coaches that carried the famous Melton Mowbray pork pies to London from 1831.

The Market Place, 1916. On the right is Warner's pie shop and café. In the centre background is Hunters The Teamen Ltd in the Market Place.

## PARKS & FAIRS

Egerton Park, *c.* 1920. The park was owned by the Wilton family who allowed it to be used as a public park from the late nineteenth century. It was purchased by the Town Estate from Lady Wilton's estate in 1931 for £1,400.

The Play Close, *c.* 1910. The close was purchased in 1856 from Lord Melbourne for the Town Estate by W.T. Tuxford and T. Ward who lent the trust the sum of £170. It has been extended by purchase and gift throughout the last 150 years. Interestingly, the Town Estate purchased part of the Melton canal site in 1886.

The bandstand in the Play Close, *c.* 1910. Shortly after it was erected extensive alterations were made to the bandstand between 1907 and 1909, when the town wardens were Henry Wood and R.W. Brownlow.

## MELTON SHOW

The Melton Show in the Market Place, May 2001. Today a gathering such as this is referred to locally as the Melton Show. The first fair or show was started in 1855 as the 'Wool Fair', which in later years became the 'Melton New Spring Fair'.

The King's Division Waterloo Band marching in the Play Close, producing stirring music, May 2001.

A 'Red Devil' from the Parachute Regiment descending on to the Play Close with St Mary's Tower in the background, May 2001.

The bandstand with a Caribbean steel band in the Play Close, 2001.

The Royal Artillery Flying Gunners Motorcycle Display Team performing on the Play Close, 2001.

Gladiators in chariots performing in the Play Close, 2001. These stunt riders are part of Tony Smart's Roman Chariot Racing Team.

'All the fun of the fair' at the Melton Show in Egerton Park, May 2001. Georgina is enjoying the roundabout and slide. The park displayed a fantastic collection of exhibits, side-shows and 'market stalls'. It is estimated that this free show attracted over sixty thousand visitors.

## STILTON & PORK PIE

Stilton cheese was originally developed in the village of Wymondham in the sixteenth century. From the early eighteenth century it was known as Stilton cheese after the town, now in Cambridgeshire, on which its marketing was centred. This is Simon Procter of Tuxford and Tebbutt, the only dairy producing Stilton cheese in Melton Mowbray. Tuxford and Tebbutt were awarded the Easom Bowl for the best Stilton cheese at the Melton Mowbray Fat Stock Show, December 2001.

The Melton Mowbray pork pie. In 1831 Edward Adcock opened a bakery in Leicester Street to produce a hand-raised pork pie from fresh, locally produced pork. He named it the Melton Mowbray pork pie. He entered into a business arrangement with the proprietor of the Leeds to London stage coach, who conveyed quantities of his pork pies to London on a daily basis. Ian Heircock was awarded the Roper Champion Cup for the finest hand-raised Melton Mowbray pork pie at the Melton Mowbray Fat Stock Show for two years running, in December 2000 and 2001. Ian is a master pie maker!

## MELTON MOWBRAY FARMERS' MARKET

Melton Mowbray Farmers' Market is held in this fine market on Tuesday and Friday mornings, when local produce is on offer. It is supported by Melton Borough Council. There is also a Tuesday market and the Sunday morning car boot/collectors' market.

A display of garden and household plants on sale.

Ann Glenn selling garden furniture in the market. For further reading on the historic town of Melton Mowbray see: *The Melton Mowbray Album*, 2001; *Leicestershire Memories*, 1999; *Melton Mowbray to Oakham*, 1998; *The History of the Melton Mowbray Pork Pie*, 1997; *The History of Stilton Cheese*, 2001 and *The Best of East Leicestershire & Rutland*, 2001.

## BURROUGH-ON-THE-HILL

An engraving of Burrough-on-the-Hill, viewed from the Leicester road, drawn on 8 September 1722 by J. Stukeley and engraved by E. Kirkall.

An engraving of 'The Hill' in 1796 from a drawing by John Trailby.

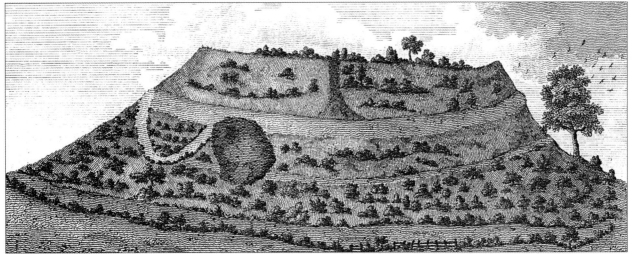

A view of the hill in March 2002 with Georgina and Chloé preparing to advance on the hill from the Little Dalby road.

The hillside of the historic site at Burrough. On 6 April 1895 Lord Lonsdale of Barleythorpe Hall near Oakham organised a point-to-point meeting for the Army. Guest of honour was the Prince of Wales, later Edward VII. The drawings printed below were prepared for the *Daily Graphic* by Cuthbert Bradley.

*Left:* The Prince of Wales arriving at the meeting in Lord Lonsdale's carriage, displaying his famous yellow livery.

*Below:* The grandstand of Burrough-on-the-Hill. The spectators had a splendid view across the valley.

*Left:* Lord Lonsdale. He organised the layout of the course and also instructed the jockeys on the route. All the races started at the base of the Hill, and went out to Little Dalby, via Twyford, and back to Burrough. For further reading see page 36 of *Around Rutland*.

The completion of the Army point-to-point catch weight, a 12-stone race, being won by Mr B.F. Loftus of the Grenadier Guards riding his brown mare St Bridget II. Lord William Bentinck came second on Rusult, owned by Mr W. Lawson of the Scots Guards, out of twenty-four runners.

Chloé and Georgina on the toposcope, a copper-covered focal point indicating places of interest that can be seen on a clear day from this vantage point.

Georgina and Chloé walking in the small wood below the north ridge of the hill. The wood contains a maintained public footpath. In the spring the spread of bluebells under the trees is magnificent.

Visitors flying kites from the ramparts, March 2002. (For further reading consult *The Best of East Leicestershire & Rutland*.)

In the village of Burrough-on-the-Hill stands a very pleasant public house, the Stag & Hounds, seen here in January 2001. After enjoying a good walk up and around 'The Hill' rest a while in this hostelry and enjoy the locally cooked food that is on offer. (For further reading see page 58 of *Leicestershire Memories*.)

Sunday lunch at the Stag & Hounds, December 2001. Left to right: Amy, Chloé, Georgina, Sharon, Pam, Simon and me.

## CARNEGIE MUSEUM

The Carnegie Free Library, 1914. This building was opened as the town museum in 1977. With Heritage Lottery Funding and considerable financial support from the Museum of Hunting Trust, Melton Borough Council and the Friends of Leicestershire Museums, the museum was reopened on Friday 3 May 2002. Fine exhibits record the heritage of the town and show the three main interests that have made the town famous internationally: fox hunting, cheese manufacture and the production of the famous local pork pie.

A display from Rowells shop in the 1930s featuring shoes and boots for the fox-hunting fraternity.

Melton Mowbray pork pies: a display of memorabilia.

A cheese cover depicting the Bell Inn at Stilton, with a complete baby Stilton cheese.

Steel hoops are used to produce Stilton cheese. These have been manufactured by a local tinsmith. They are arranged on Frank Fryer's hastener. The lead for consolidating the curd, with the plug in situ for draining out the whey, can be seen in the foreground.

'The tinsmith's workshop' was donated to the town museum by the Coy family from Harby, who were tin- and lead-smiths in the village from the late nineteenth century until the 1960s.

# 4

# *Battle Plains*

The ruins of Kirby Muxloe Castle in a lithograph drawn on stone and printed by John Flower, *c.* 1820. It is a brick-built structure constructed to a design by Lord Hastings of Ashby Castle; building commenced in about 1480. In 1483 Hastings was summarily beheaded on the orders of Richard III. Only a few miles away is Bosworth Field, the site of the famous last battle of the Wars of the Roses, where Richard III was killed in 1485. After the battle his naked body was carried on the back of a horse to Leicester to be displayed in the town. Henry Tudor was crowned king on Redmore Plain with Richard's crown that was found in a bush near Stoke Golding. This site is still known as Crown Hill. The small town of Market Bosworth is always worth visiting, especially on market day. There are some interesting small shops and nice public houses. A trip to Twycross Zoo, on the edge of the county on the Warwickshire border, makes a fine day out. The zoo specialises in breeding endangered species. Many of the animals in the zoo are close to extinction, and a unique breeding programme has resulted in some remarkable achievements.

## MARKET BOSWORTH

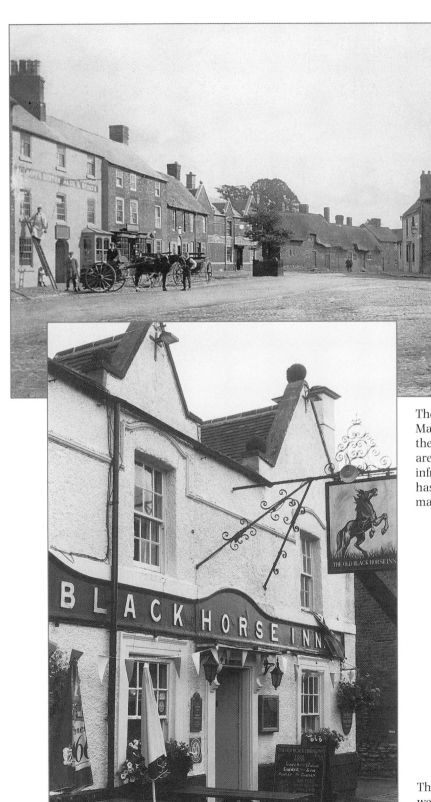

The Black Horse Inn in the market place, Market Bosworth, 1904. The landlord of the pub was Joseph Palmer. Today this area is very restricted: cars are parked infront of the inn and a war memorial has been erected in the centre of the market place.

The 'Old' Black Horse Inn, 2002. It is well worth a visit to enjoy a light lunch in historic surroundings.

Market Bosworth station, 1903. Opened on 1 September 1873 on the Ashby and Nuneaton joint line, it closed on 13 April 1931. The stationmaster, Ellis Bray, is possibly the person standing in front of the window to the right, next to the station porter.

Sir Alexander Beaumont Churchill Dixie, of Bosworth Park, 1895.

A Midland Longhorn on display at the Bosworth show in the park at Market Bosworth, 1903.

Half-timbered cottages on Sutton Lane, Market Bosworth, 1903.

Half-timbered cottages viewed from the Market Square, 2002.

Ye Olde Red Lion Hotel on Park Street, Market Bosworth, 2002.

Near the Black Horse Inn is a very interesting walkway leading to a selection of very small local shops. Sweet Companions Book Shop, containing a selection of local history books, is well worth a visit.

After visiting the bookshop enjoy some refreshments at The Victorian Tea Parlour.

## BOSWORTH FIELD

Whitemoors Antiques and Crafts Centre with licensed tea rooms is within spear-throwing distance of the very spot where King Richard III fell at the Battle of Bosworth.

A fingerpost erected in Bosworth Field. Over the last 200 years considerable comment has been published on the exact site of the Battle of Bosworth Field. In 1813 John Nichols updated and published W. Hutton's book *Bosworth Field* with newly commissioned engravings. According to maps published in the eighteenth century the site was centred on the villages of Shenton, Market Bosworth, Sutton Cheyney, Stapleton and Dadlington. This is an area of low hills and marshland. Historians in the twenty-first century disagreed with John Nichols about the site of the battle. Does it really matter? This is a splendid site, and our ancestors thought it was the correct site – 'so be it'.

This field is presumed by many historians to be the place where King Richard III was killed in 1485.

King Richard III (1483–85). A formidable warrior during his short reign, he ruled England with a rod of iron and attempted to kill all his enemies. In 1484 his son died and then his Queen died the year after. He ran the country with his hated lieutenants, Catesby, Ratcliffe and Lovell under the flag of the wild boar. Hence the doggerel rhyme,

King Henry VII (1485–1509). Henry defeated Richard III on Bosworth Field. Although he had a very weak hereditary claim to the throne, he gained his crown through victory on the battlefield. He was an astute king, and for a quarter of a century ruled wisely. He left a prosperous country to his son Henry VIII.

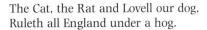

The Cat, the Rat and Lovell our dog,
Ruleth all England under a hog.

King Richard's well, 1925. Local folklore dictates that this is the well where Richard quenched his thirst during the battle. In 1813 Samuel Parr, a county historian, paid for the building of this cairn over the well. It is now maintained by the Fellowship of the White Boar. In the background stands the farmhouse that has been converted into the Bosworth battlefield visitors' centre.

Bosworth battlefield visitors' centre, 2002. This building contains a tourist shop, museum and tea room.

Sutton Cheyney Wharf on the Ashby Canal, with the Wharf House tea room in the centre background, 2002. Take a circular walk through Ambion Wood to this wharf, stop for refreshment, then complete the walk; this route is clearly marked with fingerposts.

The disused railway bridge that is now on the footpath in Ambion Wood, 2002. At this point the route follows the Ashby Canal. The canal barge passing under the steel railway bridge is carrying passengers from Sutton Cheyney Wharf.

HINCKLEY

Coventry Road, Hinckley, 1791, in an engraving from a drawing by J. Walker. This was a rural market town. Today it has a very fine market and an interesting shopping complex. In the background stands the Church of St Mary, well worth visiting to view the memorials.

Simkin & James, grocers and wine and spirit merchants, Market Place, Hinckley, 1904. Compare this carriers' wagon with the one on page 56. A similar wagon is on display at the Snibston Museum.

John Groom's Crippleage and Flower Girls' Mission, Drill Hall, Hinckley, 12 June 1911.

The Market Place, Hinckley, 2002. Traditionally a market is held every Monday. On every third Thursday in the month a farmers' market is held in the Market Place, retailing quality local produce.

The Borough, Hinckley, *c.* 1930.

The war memorial on the site of Hinckley Castle, 2002. Part of the moat, ramparts and remains of the walls of the castle are still visible. This fortress was demolished during the Wars of the Roses.

## HINCKLEY MUSEUM

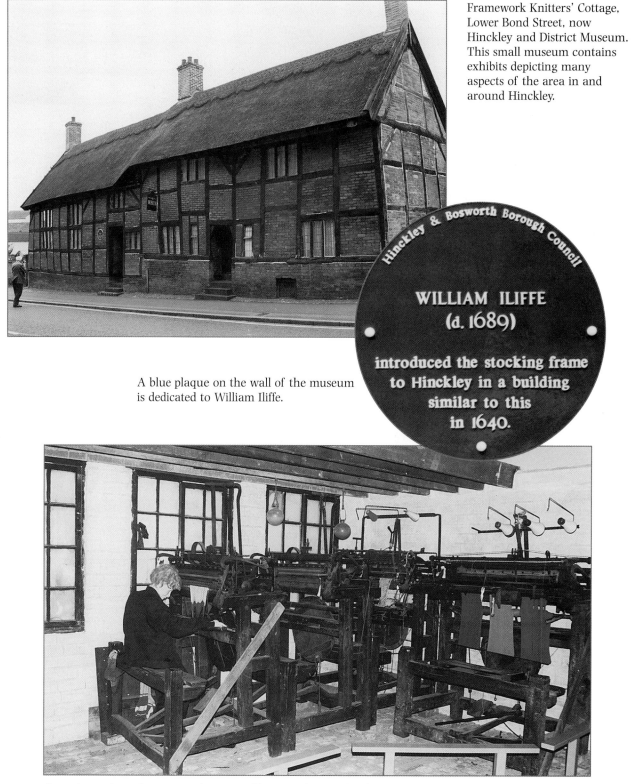

Framework Knitters' Cottage, Lower Bond Street, now Hinckley and District Museum. This small museum contains exhibits depicting many aspects of the area in and around Hinckley.

Hinckley & Bosworth Borough Council

WILLIAM ILIFFE
(d. 1689)

introduced the stocking frame
to Hinckley in a building
similar to this
in 1640.

A blue plaque on the wall of the museum is dedicated to William Iliffe.

A stockinger's work room, with a typical knitting frame. This frame is on display in Snibston Museum.

## TWYCROSS

Bornean orang-utans playing happily together. They are fascinated by the activities of the visitors viewing them from outside the enclosure. In the wild these animals live solitary lives in the jungle. They are an endangered species.

Humboldt penguins, another endangered species, being fed. The breeding birds can be viewed from an underwater walk after their feed of fish.

Visitors in the adventure playground. Compare the young orang-utans with these children at play!

Asian elephants are breeding very successfully at Twycross.

A giraffe finishing off its daily offering of leafed twigs and branches.

Asiatic lions. As terrible as it sounds, there is a strong possibility that these splendid animals will not survive in the wild. Only zoological trusts such as Twycross can keep this species from extinction. Eventually the lions will be returned to havens in the wild that are permanently protected.

Scarlet macaws, magnificent parrots found in the forests of Central and South America, are under threat from loggers.

A white cockatoo is a fine pet for this zoo. Native to Australia, New Guinea and neighbouring islands, it has been introduced into New Zealand.

A selection of South American animals: alpaca and mara are in the foreground. Capybara, the world's largest rodent, a type of guinea pig the size of a sheep, can also be seen.

Asian short-clawed otters at play.

Standing in front of the Langur house are the Grech family, visiting tourists from Malta, in the summer of 1999. Back row, left to right: Norman, Sharon, Edith. Front row: Chloé, Georgina, Beverly.

Children on the slide in the adventure playground, 2002. Georgina is enjoying herself.

## BATTLEFIELD LINE

Shackerstone station, June 2002. The station was opened on
1 September 1873 on the Ashby and Nuneaton joint line and closed on
13 April 1931 when the railway was amalgamated with the LMS.

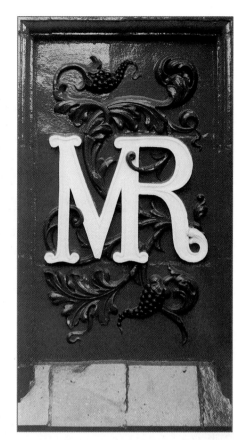

A Midland Railway design on display at this working museum.

Rolling stock on the track at Shackerstone.

Shackerstone, 2002. Most weekends and on
certain days during the summer months it is
possible to take a 10-mile journey on one of the
restored trains operating out of this station
through the beautiful rolling countryside of south-
west Leicestershire to Shenton station.

## KIRBY MUXLOE

Kirby Muxloe Castle, 1796. The brick-built structure was produced to a design recommended by Lord Hastings of Ashby Castle.

Kirby Muxloe Castle, *c.* 1900.

Restoration of the castle taking place in the 1920s.

Kirby Muxloe Castle, the entrance gateway, *c.* 1930.

The moat and west tower of Kirby Muxloe Castle, *c.* 1930.

The main street in the village of Kirby Muxloe, 1905. Stabling is on offer on the right at the Royal Oak public house, of which the landlord was Philip Bosworth. The building by the entrance to the public house was demolished and it now forms the driveway to the new Royal Oak.

## BRUNTINGTHORPE

Bruntingthorpe Aerodrome was built between 1941 and 1943. It was the home of 92 Group Bomber Command during the Second World War, and during the Cold War in the 1960s and 1970s it was a major strategic aerodrome. In the 1990s, after much discussion, it became a major force in aircraft preservation. A Hawker Sea Hawk and two English Electric Lightnings in line behind can be seen above.

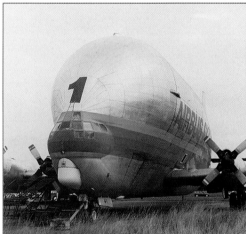

Boeing Super Guppy No. 1, Airbus Skylink. Eventually this vast aeroplane will be the centre's museum.

The famous Vulcan being restored in its hanger with Denis Parker, Support Services, and Rusty Drewett, PA and Engineering Director.

## ASHBY CANAL

Canal Wharf, Stoke
Golding, on the
Ashby Canal, June
2002.

THE CHARITY OF THOMAS BARTON

THE
ASHBY DE LA ZOUCH
CANAL
Opened in 1804
it connected the
Ashby Woulds Coalfield
with the Coventry Canal
at Marston Junction

800TH ANNIVERSARY 10TH JULY 2000

A blue plaque on the wall of a cottage at the wharf
commemorates the opening of the canal in 1804.

CHANDLERY   RECEPTION   SOUVENIR

Open

OPENING HOURS
MON - SAT - 8.30am - 5.00pm
Summer (April - Oct)
SUNDAY - 9.00am - 1.00pm
Winter - (Nov - March)
SUNDAY - CLOSED

The chandlery of
the Ashby Boat
Co., Canal Wharf,
Stoke Golding. It
is possible to hire
a canal boat for
short journeys or
for longer periods
from this
chandlery.

The canal boat *Rose* moored at Sutton Cheney Wharf on the Ashby Canal, June 2002.

*Rose* is run by Sue and Bill Jeffery, along with their sister-boat *Rosebud*, which is suitable for short, one-hour trips. On *Rose* it is possible to dine, and fine meals are available. Lorna Maybery has just taken her seat and is contemplating the menu prior to ordering her Sunday lunch afloat, June 2002.

# 5

# *Canals & Scholars*

The Free Grammar School, founded by Robert Smyth in 1614. This engraving was produced in about 1789 by Rowland Royse, and was published in 1808. In the centre of Market Harborough this spectacular building dominates the town. Visit the Harborough Museum to the rear of the council offices. This museum holds a very fine collection of local history. To the north of Market Harborough lies Foxton Locks on the Grand Union Canal. There is considerable interest in the use and expansion of the canal network through England, not least at Foxton Locks, opened in 1812. Plans are in progress to rebuild the inclined plane, a powered boat-lift. Foxton Locks provide an impressive rise of 75ft. The small town of Lutterworth is worth a visit, especially the Church of St Mary the Virgin. In this church John Wycliffe, the fourteenth-century English reformer, is remembered. Visit Stanford Hall on the north bank of the River Avon; the village of Stanford on the south bank of the river is in Northamptonshire. The Hall is open to the public. The church in the village is worth visiting and has a splendid display of memorials.

## MARKET HARBOROUGH

Market Harborough from the south in an engraving published in 1792, featuring a packhorse bridge with a ford across the River Welland. A carrier's cart is travelling into the market town. Dominating this view is the splendid steeple of the Church of St Dionysius.

In 1720 the very first road atlas was published to be carried in pouches or pockets, principally by horse riders delivering the mail. The first engraving in any atlas detailing the 'pony express' featured this market town as little more than a village with a stone bridge, 84 miles north of London. It was an important route because if the Welland was in flood there was a soundly constructed six-arched bridge at 'Haverborough'.

Smith's Charity School, opened in 1614, in the 1920s. This unique, historic building stands proudly in the centre of the town.

A view of the canal at Market Harborough, *c.* 1910. This extension of the Grand Union Canal from Foxton Locks has been used for pleasure boating since the late nineteenth century. It was completed as far as the wharf at Market Harborough by 1809.

The canal basin with the nineteenth-century warehouse, 2002. Plans had been laid out to connect this basin, via the River Welland, through to Stamford. However, the railway boom put an end to this idea.

Market Harborough canal basin at the end of the Grand Union extension into the town, 2002. It is now a twenty-first-century marina enjoying considerable development of canal-side properties, with a charming waterside walk through to Foxton.

Leicester Road, Market Harborough, 1904. In the background stands the splendid steeple of the Church of St Dionysius. The vicar was the Revd Robert Guinness MA, who was also rural dean to the Gartree Hundred.

One of the finest hotels in Leicestershire, the Three Swans on High Street. It was first recorded as a hostelry in the town in 1517.

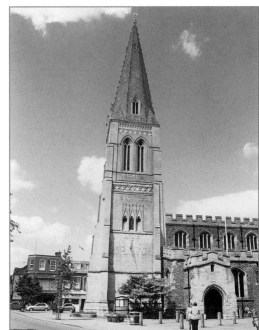

The magnificent spire of the Church of St Dionysius dominates the centre of the town. The church contains a fine display of local church history.

The Square, Market Harborough, before the First World War, *c.* 1910.

A similar view to the one above, 6 August 1914. These are some of the 2,000 Market Harborough men who volunteered to fight in the First World War.

Market Harborough cattle market, *c.* 1912. This market was opened in 1903. In the background are the 'settling rooms' where the market returns were paid out. During the first two years of trading almost 100,000 head of cattle and sheep were sold.

A splendid view of The Square and Station Road, 1905. Horse-drawn vehicles and a flock of eight sheep enliven the view.

Farmers' market, 2002.

## HARBOROUGH MUSEUM

Reconstructed boot and shoe workshop in the museum. The museum entrance is on Fox Yard. On the first floor are the Harborough District Council Offices, originally the Symington Corset Factory.

A 100-year-old ash bucket lavatory that was used at Church Langton. A unique system released a quantity of ashes into the bucket under the seat.

A permanent display that is part of the historic Symington Corset Factory. Jane Tugwell demonstrates part of the machine-sewing system.

## LUTTERWORTH

The Wycliffe Memorial, erected to celebrate Queen Victoria's Diamond Jubilee in 1897. This monument stands on the junction of the Coventry and Bitteswell road in front of the Methodist church, built in 1905.

John Wycliffe, *c.* 1320–84, was a church reformer. He was appointed rector of Lutterworth in 1374 and died from a fatal stroke on New Year's Eve, 1384. He published the first translation of the Bible from Latin into English. His statue stands over the entrance to Leicester Cathedral: see page 59 of *The Best of Leicester*.

'The Morning Star'. Wycliffe's bones were exhumed and burnt on a fire in 1428 and the ashes thrown into the River Swift, a tributary of the Avon, which spread his remains, via the sea, all over the world!

The Avon to the Severn runs.
The Severn to the Sea.
And Wycliff's dust shall spread abroad.
Wide the waters be!

The Church of St Mary
the Virgin, 1925, when
the rector was the Revd
Canon Walter Paton
Hinckley MA. On the left
stands the Coach and
Horses public house, the
landlady of which was
Mrs Thomas Wells.

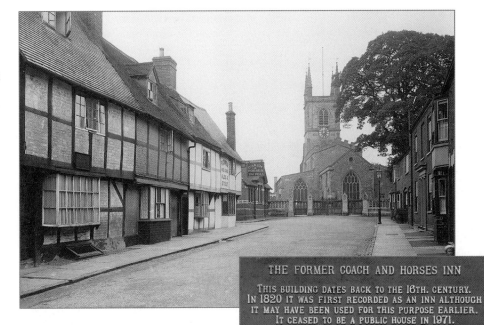

The Coach and Horses is no longer an inn. This plaque
was attached to the building in 1977.

THE FORMER COACH AND HORSES INN

THIS BUILDING DATES BACK TO THE 16TH. CENTURY.
IN 1820 IT WAS FIRST RECORDED AS AN INN ALTHOUGH
IT MAY HAVE BEEN USED FOR THIS PURPOSE EARLIER.
IT CEASED TO BE A PUBLIC HOUSE IN 1971.

BUILT ORIGINALLY AS AN OAK—FRAMED BUILDING WITH
WATTLE AND DAUB WALLS WITH ITS FIRST FLOOR
JETTIED OUT OVER THE FOOTPATH, IT WAS ACQUIRED BY
THE LUTTERWORTH RURAL DISTRICT COUNCIL IN 1972.

THE RESTORATION WAS PLANNED IN 1975 AS THE
HARBOROUGH DISTRICT COUNCIL'S CONTRIBUTION TO
EUROPEAN ARCHITECTURAL HERITAGE YEAR, AND THE
CONVERSION TO TWO DWELLINGS WAS COMPLETED
IN DECEMBER, 1976.

THE TIMBERED PROPERTY ADJACENT WAS ALSO
RENOVATED BY THE LOCAL AUTHORITY IN 1968/9.

THIS PLAQUE WAS PROVIDED IN 1977 BY
HARBOROUGH DISTRICT COUNCIL

1952          1977

COMMEMORATING THE SILVER JUBILEE OF
THE ACCESSION OF H.M. QUEEN ELIZABETH II

A terracotta dog looks out on to Market Street from its
perch above the late Victorian doorway on the corner of
Church Street. This is an area of interesting small shops,
not least a bookshop selling local history books.

The bust of Sir Frank Whittle, erected at the corner of the Memorial Gardens on Church Street. Frank Whittle pioneered the design of the jet engine in 1936. Most of his design work was undertaken from 1938 to 1941 in a foundry on Leicester Road in Lutterworth. The first jet-engined aeroplane, the Gloster E28/39, took off on 14 May 1941.

The Shambles public house on Bell Street, off Market Street. This building dates from the sixteenth century. It stands on the site of the Beast Market, where slaughtered cattle and farm animals were sold.

Lutterworth Town Museum on Church Gate was built in 1876 as the reading room. The museum holds a collection of artefacts from the town's past.

STANFORD HALL

Stanford Hall, 8 January 1992, with Jeremy Reed, the Pytchley whipper-in, leading the Pytchley Foxhounds through the gate at the meet.

The rose garden at Stanford Hall, August 2002. The hall contains a fine collection of antiques and pictures. The stable block houses a motorcycle collection, a craft centre and tea room.

The blacksmith's shop at Stanford Hall, 2002.

The tomb of Sir Thomas and Lady Cave in the Church of St Nicholas. This small church stands over the Leicestershire border in Northamptonshire, in the village of Stanford-on-Avon, and is well worth visiting. Caves and Verdens are well represented, with some excellent monuments depicting the long-dead occupants of Stanford Hall across the river.

## PERCY PILCHER

The Percy Pilcher Museum has been laid out in the stable block at Stanford Hall. Percy was England's pioneer aviator in the nineteenth century, and he flew and researched his aeroplanes in the park at Stanford. In the museum is a replica of the Hawk that Lieutenant Pilcher RN flew for four years. He was developing a tri-plane powered by an engine at the time he was killed in the Hawk.

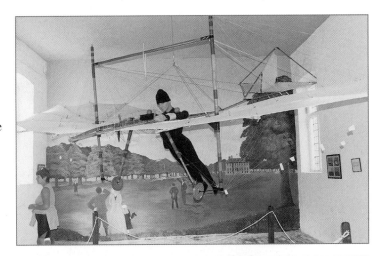

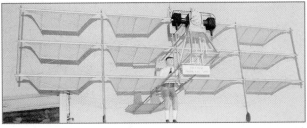

A replica of Pilcher's tri-plane.

Percy Pilcher crashed and was killed in a field near Stanford Hall on 30 September 1899. This monument was erected by the Royal Aeronautical Society at the place he was killed.

*Right:* If this pioneer of English aviation had lived, unquestionably he would have flown the first engine-powered aeroplane. *Icaro Alteri*, which means 'the other Icarus', is inscribed on the reverse of this monument.

## FOXTON LOCKS

Foxton Locks, *c.* 1920. The locks were completed in 1812 after the Market Harborough line had been opened in 1809. The original idea was to connect Leicester with Northampton, via Market Harborough, to broadbeam dimensions. However, the company ran out of capital, so the scheme was put on hold. Fortunately, a new company was formed with new money. In the end 23 miles of canal were built with the narrowbeam locks at Foxton allowing a rise of 75ft.

*Left:* Negotiating the locks with Foxton Boat Services public house in the background (see page 147).

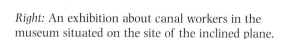

*Right:* An exhibition about canal workers in the museum situated on the site of the inclined plane.

Foxton Locks, with the lock-keeper's cottage on the top of the hill, October 1907.

Foxton's inclined steam-powered boat-lift. This lift was opened on 10 July 1900 to help the canal compete with various railway companies for trade. It was not successful. The locks were reopened and the pair of boat-lifts were mothballed in 1911 and demolished in 1928. A scrap merchant paid the sum of £250 for the privilege. The original scheme cost £37,500. There are plans to rebuild this inclined plane in the near future – at what cost?

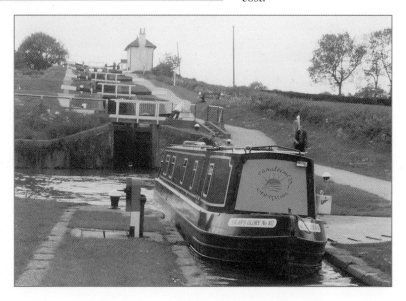

*Aslan's Glory*, No. 102, leaving the passing point, descending the system of locks to bridge No. 62.

Don standing on the service bridge at the chamber, which consists of two staircases and two locks.

The cast-iron notice providing information about bridge No. 63 to Foxton village.

MOTOR CAR ACTS
1896 AND 1903

NOTICE.
This
BRIDGE
Is insufficient to carry a
HEAVY MOTOR CAR
The Registered Axle weight of any axle of which exceeds
3 TONS
or the Registered Axle-Weights of the several
axles of which exceed in the aggregate
5 TONS
or a Heavy Motor Car drawing a
TRAILER
if the Registered Axle Weights of the several Axles
of the HEAVY MOTOR CAR and the
Axle Weights of the several Axles of the
TRAILER
Exceed in the aggregate
5 TONS

OXFORD CANAL NAVIGATION

OXFORD

Bridge No. 62 with Foxton Boat Services in the background.

The boat yard at Foxton, on the junction of the
Foxton to Market Harborough arm.

Public house at bridge No. 61, adjacent to the
Foxton Boat Services. In the foreground a sign on
*Vixen* advertises horse-drawn trips.

A collection of boats waiting to descend the Foxton locks. The locks have never been busier. During
bank holidays boats can queue for up to five hours before entering the system.

## HALLATON

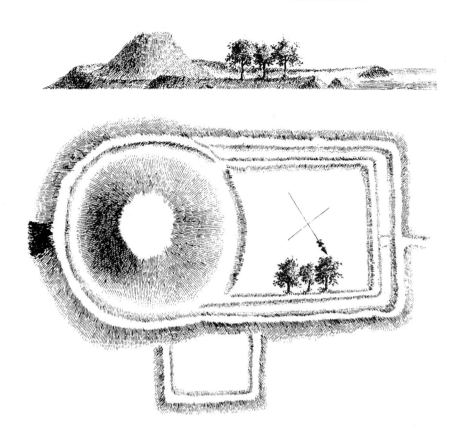

The village of Hallaton is situated in the south-east corner of the county. In the twelfth century it was dominated by a small motte and bailey castle, certainly constructed to defend the extensive iron-ore workings in the vicinity. The site of the castle lies to the west of the village near a stream on the side of a hill, built on the edge of a sunken road that served the iron-ore workings. This engraving was published in 1795. Extensive archaeological excavations took place here in 1878.

Hallaton from the vicinity of the castle with St Michael and All Angels' Church in the background. This drawing was produced by J.P. Malcolm in 1793 and published as an engraving by John Nichols.

Church Street and St Michael and All Angels in a photograph taken by Fred Hawke in 1904. Before the First World War Fred published a marvellous collection of postcards and other productions featuring Hallaton and the surrounding villages. When it is open, visit the Hallaton Museum, Hog Lane, Hallaton, LE16 8UE.

The unusual fifteenth-century market cross, the Butter Cross, before the First World War. Permission to hold a market on this site was granted by Henry II in 1224. The market died out in the 1830s because of the growth of the town market at nearby Market Harborough.

The Fernie Hunt in Hallaton in the 1920s, when Lord Stalbridge was the Master of the Hunt. The kennels were at Medbourne; they were later transferred to Great Bowden.

The start of the world-famous Hallaton Hare Pie Scrambling and Bottle Kicking, Easter Monday, 1905. The vicar is guarding the hare pie. This is an event steeped in history and probably stems from a pagan spring rite. Sample some pie! Fight for a bottle! Two villages fight for the bottles, Hallaton and nearby Medbourne.

The curate, Harry Neal, cutting up the hare pie which will be placed in the sack to be distributed to the participants of the bottle-kicking, prior to the general fracas on Stowe Hill, 1904.

Celebrations at the Butter Cross, *c.* 1920. Once more Hallaton has successfully defended the brook between the two villages below Stowe Hill. Medbourne first recorded a win in the contest in 1936.

## MEDBOURNE

An engraving, published in the 1790s, of the picturesque setting of the Church of St Giles with the packhorse bridge across the stream and moat.

The tower of the Church of St Giles, 1904. The vicar was the Revd Charles Fryer Eastburn MA. The packhorse bridge is clearly shown in line with the tower. The church was fortified during the reign of King Stephen (1135–54) as the countryside was dominated by marauding barons. The moat would have offered some defence against casual mercenaries, but would not have lasted long against a well-designed siege.

Footbridge and ford across the Medbourne Brook in the 1920s. Medbourne is a picturesque village near the River Welland. When visiting this district, visit some of the very pleasant public houses and enjoy the food and drink in the restaurants that these hostelries offer.

## EYE BROOK

Eye Brook rises out of the southern ridge of Tilton-on-the-Hill, draining through the countryside to the River Welland at Caldecott in Rutland. This reservoir was built by Stewarts and Lloyds to supply water to their steel works in Corby, completed in 1940. The Eye Brook is also the boundary between Leicestershire and Rutland. This is a view from the Rutland side, 2002. This expanse of water is a haven for wild fowl. Laybys have been built off the highway at regular intervals to enable visitors who come by car to view this interesting expanse of water.

Fishing for trout on this reservoir is highly recommended. This is a view from the Leicestershire bank of the reservoir with the fields near Stoke Dry in Rutland in the background. During numerous moonlit nights in April 1943 the valley vibrated to the noise of Lancaster bombers practising for the daring bombing raids on the dams in Germany in May, sights being taken across the surface water to line up with the dam wall.

## LAUNDE ABBEY

An engraving of Launde Abbey, published in the 1790s. An Augustinian priory was founded on this site in 1119 and dissolved by Henry VIII in 1538. Of the original building only the chancel remains, now the chapel. Thomas Cromwell was granted this priory and its estates by Henry VIII. His family built a mansion on the site of the dissolved building. Considerable alterations have taken place since then and today much of the building is seventeenth century.

Launde Abbey. A laund or lawn is a large area of pasture land used for rearing sheep in large unenclosed fields. See page 85 in *The History of Stilton Cheese*.

Welcome to

# Launde Abbey

## THE CHURCH OF ENGLAND

Leicester Diocesan Retreat House and Conference Centre

## The Chapel is Open to Members of the Public at Certain Times, Please Telephone The Abbey for Details
Tel:- (01572) 717254   Fax:- (01572) 717454

An advertisement for Launde Abbey, 2002. The tomb of Gregory, Lord Cromwell, is worth viewing in the chapel at the abbey. It is dated 1551.

HALSTEAD FARM

Halstead Farm, March 2002. This is a working farm, not a museum or a collection of animals.

The entrance to Halstead Farm. Note the cobbled road to the nineteenth-century farmstead.

Myles with his dad Ian, looking at the two sows and the boar.

Angela explaining to Ianthe that these are two pigs!

Harriet and Myles in the stack yard. The children's toys reflect a farming influence – two tractors!

Occasionally rides on the farm pony can be arranged. Here, in March 2002, Ian is adjusting a stirrup for Harriet, and Myles is waiting his turn for a ride on the pony with Tara Derry. In the background can be seen some of the farm's cattle. There are some fine footpaths around the farm, where it is possible to look at the variety of farm animals.

Denzil the llama, the farm pet.

A big fat boar with visitors.

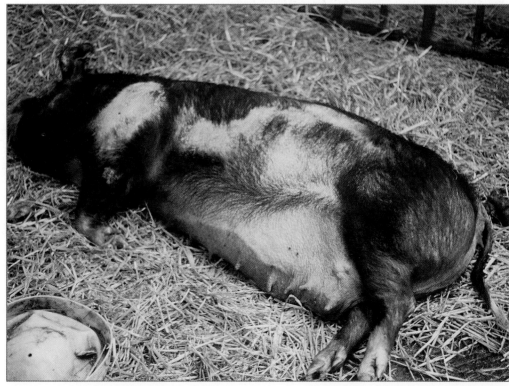

Typical! – a well-fed Gloucester Old Spot pig sleeping on a bed of straw.

# BIBLIOGRAPHY

Andrews, W., *Bygone Leicestershire*, 1892

Baker, D., Clamp, C. and Duckworth, S., *Images of England: Coalville*, 1998

Baresiner, Y., *British County Maps*, 1983

Beaumont, P., *History of the Moira Collieries*, 1919

Bonser, R., *Aviation in Leicestershire and Rutland*, 2001

Bowen, E., *Britannia Depicta*, 1720

Bryant, A., *1000 Years in Leicestershire and Rutland*, 2001

Flower, J., *Views of the Ancient Buildings in the Town and County of Leicester*, 1826

Hadfield, C., *The Canals of the East Midlands*, 1966

Harrod, W., *Market Harborough*, 1808

Hextall, W. and J. (eds), *The History and Description of Ashby-de-la-Zouch*, 1852

Hillier, K., *Around Ashby-de-la-Zouch in Old Photographs*, 1994

Hoskins, W.G., *Leicestershire*, 1970

Kelly, W., *Royal Progress and Visits to Leicester*, 1884

*Kelly's Directory, Leicestershire and Rutland*, 1900, 1904, 1916, 1925, 1941

Kelsey, C.E., *Leicestershire*, 1915

McWhirr, A., *Sycamore Leaves*, 1985

Mastoris, S., *Around the Welland Valley*, 1991

Moon, N., *Leicestershire and Rutland Windmills*, 1981

Morrison, J. and Daisley, R., *Hallaton, Hare Pie Scramblings and Bottle Kicking*, 2000

Musters, C., *A Cavalier Stronghold*, 1890

Nichols, J., *The History and Antiquities of the County of Leicester* (4 vols in 8), 1795–1811

Pearson, M., *Pearson's Canal Companion: East Midlands*, 1997

Pearson, M., *Pearson's Canal Companion: South Midlands*, 1997

Press, T. (ed.), *Nottingham, Leicestershire and Rutland*, 1895

Read, M. (ed.), *One Hundred Favourite Poems*, 2000

Spencer, J. and T. (eds), *Leicester and Rutland, Notes and Queries* (3 vols), 1891–5

*Spencers' Almanack*, 1901

Stevenson, J., *A Family Guide to Bradgate Park and Swithland Wood*, 1979

Wix, D., Shacklock, P. and Keil, I., *The River Soar in Old Photographs*, 1992

# ACKNOWLEDGEMENTS

To produce such a book as this requires considerable research over many years. For most of my working life I have been interested in the history of the county of Leicestershire. During the last half of the twentieth century considerable changes have taken place, particularly in the industrial operations in the countryside, such as open-cast sites and coal mining. Much of the industrial landscape has been changed to take in tourism. In this book I have attempted to record much of the historic past and the change to commercial tourism. To put together this collection of photographs and illustrations I have needed the help of many people.

I gratefully thank the following for their help: Tim Williams; Doris Green; Alan Salt; Mark Bowen; Stephen Hallam; Don Humberston; Jo Humberston; John Baker-Courtenay; Tom Wheatcroft; Jenny Dancey; and Jenny Moore, Maureen Hallahan and Heather Broughton of Leicestershire County Council, Museums, Arts and Record Services.

Thanks must also go to all those people whom I met on my journey during 2001 and 2002 and who gave me information and advice about this most interesting county. Many hours were spent with Don Humberston, whose knowledge of the Leicestershire countryside was invaluable. His experience of tracks and minor roads is remarkable, and led us both into some very interesting locations.

All of the historic images are out of copyright, and I hold the originals in my personal collection. The photographs on pages 69 (bottom), 82 (bottom), 101 (both), 130 (bottom) and on the back cover were provided by Tim Williams, who has given me permission to print them but retains the copyright. I retain the copyright of all the other photographs. Once again I must thank Pat Peters for processing the manuscript to enable Sutton Publishing to release the third volume in my series 'The Best Of'.

The 'Humber Stone', a large glacial boulder that was reputedly carried down to this site in the village of Humberstone by a glacier during the last Ice Age from the Humber basin. This stone is marked on the 1:50,000 Ordnance Survey map. Druids, Danes and Saxons are all said to have used this stone as a sacrificial altar.

# SELECTIVE INDEX

Abbey Park 10
Ashby Canal 7, 79, 80, 116, 129
Ashby-de-la-Zouch 6, 7, 15, 41, 42, 44, 45, 46, 58, 49, 50, 51, 74
Ashdown, Charles 49
Atherstone Hunt 31

Bakewell, Robert 28
Bannion, Charles 35
Basset Hounds 30
Beacon Hill 8, 70
Bell Foundry 7, 60, 66, 22
Belvoir Castle 7, 81, 82, 86, 90, 91
Bosworth Field 114, 115
Bradgate Park 8, 15, 35, 36, 39
Bruntingthorpe 128
Burrough-on-the-Hill 8, 81, 103, 104, 106

Canada geese 32
Carillon 7, 62, 68
castles 7, 15, 23, 24, 46, 47, 49, 81, 82, 86, 87, 89, 90, 91, 92, 109, 119, 126, 127, 148
Castle Donington 15, 16
Charnwood 60, 64
Clinch, John 9
clock tower 11
Coalville 8, 15, 51, 52, 53, 54
concerts 90, 91
Conkers 6, 7, 15, 74, 75, 76, 78, 79, 80
corn exchange 9
county show 29
Cropston reservoir 39
cupola 25

Dannatt, Trevor 13
Dishley 28, 29
Donington-le-Heath 15, 58, 59
Donington Park 16, 17, 18, 20

edge railway 92
Eye Brook 153

fallow deer 38
Ferrers Centre 73
Ferrers, Earl 71, 72
finger pillory 43
Flint, William 9

Flower, John 15, 46, 47, 81
Foxton Locks 8, 131, 133, 144, 145, 146, 147

Grand Union Canal 7, 14, 33, 131, 133, 144
granite 24
Great Central Railway 7, 15, 60, 69
great crested grebe 34
Grey Lady 40
Grey, Lady Jane 35, 36

Hallaton 148, 149, 150, 151
Halstead Farm 155, 156
hare pie 150, 151
heron 34
Hinckley 7, 117, 118, 119

Jewry Wall 13

*King Lear* 33
Kirby Muxloe 109, 126, 127

Laude Abbey 154
Leicester 7
Leicester Ram 28
Leicestershire Yeomanry 40
Light Brigade 89
Loughborough 7, 15, 60
Lutterworth 131, 138, 140

Malcolm, J.P. 35, 37, 148
mallard 34
mammoths 32
Market Bosworth 109, 110, 111, 112
Market Harborough 8, 131, 132, 133, 134, 135, 136, 149
market(s) 9, 22, 25, 41, 50, 61, 63, 95, 96, 102, 110, 117, 118, 136
Medbourne 150, 151, 152
Melton Mowbray 7, 81, 93, 94, 96, 101
Melton Mowbray pork pie 96, 101, 107
Melton Show 98
Midland Longhorn 28, 111
Midland Railway Co. 42, 125
Moira 6, 7, 15, 74, 76, 78, 79
Moira furnace 80

Mountsorrel 15, 23, 24, 25, 27, 57
museum(s) 13, 50, 64, 107, 120, 125, 128, 137, 143, 144, 149

National Forest 6, 7, 15, 75, 79
National Space Centre 14
New Walk 13

'Old John' 37

Pied Bull Hotel 21
Pilcher, Percy 143

red deer 38
Ronaldsay sheep 70
Royal Marines 31

St Botolph's Church 21
St Martins Square 12
Shackerstone 125
Shepshed 21, 22
Spring Gardens 84, 85
Snibston 8, 15, 51, 55, 56, 57, 117, 120
Stanford Hall 131, 141, 142, 143
Staunton Harold 71, 72
Stephenson(s) 55
Stilton cheese 63, 101, 108
Stoke Golding 7, 129
Sutton Cheyney 7, 114, 116, 130
swan 32, 34

Throsby, R. 36
Thurmaston 8, 33
tourists 7
Twycross Zoo 7, 109, 121, 122

vintage ploughing 31
visitors 6, 85, 116, 121, 157

Watermead Country Park 8, 15, 32
Waterside, The 26, 27
West Friesland 28
wharfs 7, 129, 130, 133
Wheatcroft, Tom 17
Whittle, Sir Frank 140
Wolsey, Thomas 10
Wycliffe, John 131, 138